Giftedness Is Not ENOUGH

Johnny Riley Jr.

DEDICATION

This book dedicated to my family and friends who supported me during this project. Thank you, Barbara, for your support and encouragement.

CONTENTS

ACKNOWLEDGMENTS

I am thankful for my mother and father, who encouraged me to push past the limits set by man and to move forward with my dreams.

Secondly, I would also like to thank my wife.
Thirdly, I would like to thank my family because I am who I am because of the DNA that runs through my body and blood.

Thank you! Dr. ID Samuel of City of HOPE Assemble Inc known as God's City in Jos Plateau State Nigeria and his team, who helped me a lot in finishing this project within the time limit.

THANKS AGAIN TO ALL WHO HELPED ME.

May GOD BLESS You
with much more than what
you have shared with me.

PREFACE

Your destiny, your potential and life's assignments are at the mercy of your character. If you are doing nothing about your character, then you are doing nothing about your destiny.

Be not deceived: evil communications corrupt good manners.

1 Corinthians 15:33

My friend. Gifts, talents, skills, degrees, mega affiliations, Gargantua connections, and colossal associations are not enough: If you are doing nothing about your character, you are doing nothing about your destiny.

Character is existing in the realm of consistent positive action or behavior. We must also understand that what would market us in this life and eternity is our character and that our character can speak for us in areas where certificates, citations, credentials, and beauty cannot speak for us.

That is why you must appreciate the necessity of character, especially as it applies to your destiny.

Character determines destiny.

Your future hangs on your nature. Samson was a man of very high and reputable destiny which was prophesied from the womb of his mother. He was filled with the Spirit of God from the womb, a Nazarite. The Spirit of God moved on him at will. As a teenager, he would tear apart a lion with his bare hands. But he was not careful, he kept running from one prostitute to another until the final one arrested him. Delilah became his disaster (Judges 16:20). Lack of character ruined his destiny.

The devil is toying with the lives of many people because of a lack of character. Your destiny, your potential and life's assignment are at the mercy of your character. If you are doing nothing about your character, then you are doing nothing about your destiny.

Beware! BECASUE, you will be GIFTED BUT STRANDED.

My counsel is, to work on your character. Character requires workmanship because we live in a world that is consistently confronting our character. We live in a generation where you need to watch your character consistently to avoid sin and a consequential eternity in hell. The Lord shall help us, in Jesus' Name.

INTRODUCTION

Giftedness is an intellectual ability significantly higher than average. It is a characteristic of students variously defined, that motivates differences in school programming. It is thought to persist as a trait into adult life, with various consequences studied in longitudinal studies of giftedness over the last century. There is no generally agreed definition of giftedness for either children or adults, but most educational Institutions' decisions on placement and most longitudinal studies which have followed individuals with an IQs in the top 2.5 per cent of the population—that is, IQs above 130.

Definitions of giftedness also vary across cultures, educational institutions, and nations.

The various definitions of intellectual giftedness include either general high ability or specific abilities. For example, by some definitions, an intellectually gifted person is talented in mathematics but is weak in the area of language. In particular, the relationship between artistic ability or musical ability and the high academic ability usually associated with high IQ scores is still being explored, with some authors referring to all those forms of high ability as "giftedness", while other authors distinguish "giftedness" from "talent". There is still much controversy and much research on the topic of how adult performance unfolds from trait differences in childhood, and what educational and other supports best help the development of adult giftedness.

Definitions

For many years, psychometricians, and psychologists, following in the footsteps of Lewis Terman in 1916, equated giftedness with high IQ. This "legacy" survives to the present day, in that giftedness and high IQ continue to be equated in some conceptions of giftedness. Since that early time, however, other researchers (e.g., Raymond Cattell, J. P. Guilford, and Louis Leon Thurstone) have argued that intellect cannot be expressed in such a unitary manner and have suggested more multifaceted approaches to intelligence.

Research conducted in the 1980s and 1990s has provided data which supports notions of multiple components of intelligence. This is particularly evident in the reexamination of "giftedness" by Sternberg and Davidson in their collection of articles Conceptions of Giftedness (1986; second edition 2005). The many different conceptions of giftedness presented, although distinct, are interrelated in several ways. Most of the investigators define giftedness in terms of multiple qualities, not all of which are intellectual. IQ scores are often viewed as inadequate measures of giftedness. Motivation, high self-concept, and creativity are key qualities in many of these broadened conceptions of giftedness.

Joseph Renzulli's (1978) "three rings" definition of giftedness is one frequently mentioned conceptualization of giftedness. Renzulli's definition, which defines gifted behaviors rather than gifted individuals, is composed of three components as follows: Gifted behavior consists of behaviors that reflect an interaction among three basic clusters of human traits—above average ability, high levels of task commitment, and high levels of creativity. Individuals capable of developing gifted behavior are those possessing or capable of developing this composite set of traits and applying them to any potentially valuable area of human performance. Persons who manifest or can develop an interaction among the three clusters require a wide variety of educational opportunities and services that are not ordinarily provided through regular instructional programs.

The term "gifted and talented" when used concerning students, children, or youth means students, children, or youth who give evidence of high-performance capability in areas such as intellectual, creative, artistic, or leadership capacity, or in specific academic fields, and who require services or activities not ordinarily provided by the school to fully develop such capabilities." "Gifted and talented student" means a child or youth who performs at or shows the potential for performing at a remarkably high level of accomplishment when compared to others of the same age, experience, or environment, and who exhibits high-performance capability in an intellectual, creative, or artistic area.

The major characteristics of these definitions are (a) the diversity of areas in which performance may be exhibited (e.g., intellectual, creativity, artistic, leadership, academically), the comparison with other groups (e.g., those in general education classrooms or of the same age, experience, or environment), and the use of terms that imply a need for development.

Thus: Your gift is the key to your lift; your talent is your ticket to the top, and your potential is your passport to your possibilities.

A man's gift maketh room for him and bringeth him before great men.

Proverbs 18:16

Think about these again. Your gift is key to your lift; your talent is your ticket to the top, and your potential is your passport to your possibilities.

Gift refers to talent or natural ability. It is synonymous with aptitude, knack, strength, endowment, potential, flair etc.

From our anchor scripture, it is clear, a man's gift makes room for him, especially at the top. A man's gift can catapult him from the bottom to the top.

Look at it again. Your gift is key to your lift; your talent is your ticket to the top, and your potential is your passport to your possibilities.

Now, our talents or gifts are not at equal levels. So, do not let anyone's feeling of intimidation or insecurity limit your capacity to manifest or express your giftedness.

The truth is, by the time we arrive in eternity, God will ask each of us, "The potentials that I, God, bypassed several people to give to you, how were they used? Did you allow them to be redundant? Did you use them to gain popularity for yourself? Or you used the gifts to expand the Kingdom of God and impact humanity?"

Beloved, you cannot place your gifts in a box and reach your destiny; you cannot store what you can do and become what you are meant to become in life. Impossible!

Today, I prophesy to you, as you determine to deploy and activate your gift, with good character, you shall move to the top in life as God has portioned that your life. In Jesus' Name.

1

GIFTEDNESS IS NOT ENOUGH

Romans 11:29 says, ***"For the gifts and calling of God are without repentance."***

"Without repentance" means that God will not change His mind about what He has called you to do. If God has called you, that calling is still there, whether you have obeyed or not. And if God gave you a gift—if He gifted you along a certain line—that gift is still there!

Paul told Timothy to "stir up" the gift that was within him, saying, "Wherefore I put thee in remembrance that thou stir up the gift of God, which is in thee by the putting on of my hands" (2 Tim. 1:6). If you want to walk out of God's plan for your life, it's time to stir up that gift within you!

In Ephesians chapter 4, we read about some of the "gifts" that God has given.

EPHESIANS 4:8,11–12.

8 Wherefore he saith, When he ascended on high, he led captivity captive and gave gifts unto men. . . .

11 And he gave some, apostles; and some, prophets; and some, evangelists; and some, pastors, and teachers; 12 For the perfecting of the saints, for the work of the ministry, for the edifying of the body of Christ.

The "gifts" in this passage refer to the fivefold ministry gifts: apostle, prophet, evangelist, pastor, and teacher. You may or may not be called to the fivefold ministry. But everyone can be involved in the ministry of the church as it is necessary and important part of the Body of Christ. And in one sense of the word, we're all called to preach.

To "preach" means to proclaim or to tell. We are all commissioned to share the Good News of the Gospel. We are all commissioned to share the facts of how Jesus reconciled us to God. We are all commissioned to be a living witness to others. Second Corinthians 5:18 says, "And all things are of God, who hath reconciled us to himself by Jesus Christ, and hath given to us the ministry of reconciliation." According to this verse, we have all been called to be in ministry—the ministry of reconciliation!

Now, there are certain pulpit ministries that God calls people to. Ephesians 4:11 tells us what those are: apostle, prophet, evangelist, pastor, and teacher. Thank God for these five ministry gifts! These are special ministry gifts that God set in the Church. Anyone who is called to full-time pulpit ministry is called in one of these areas. And a person can be called to function in more than one office.

According to Acts 13:1, Acts 14:14, and other scriptures in the New Testament, we know that Barnabas and Paul were both "prophets" and "teachers."

In other words, they were gifted by the Holy Ghost to function in both offices.

A person might not be faithful to the call of God on his or her life, but the call is still there, anyway. God does not recall the calling. So let us all obey God and answer the call!

When a person first accepts Christ, he may have such a desire to see other people saved that he starts to think, Maybe God called me to be an evangelist. That may or may not be the case. If it is the case, then obey the call.

But if it is not, you can still assist people through being a minister of reconciliation.

**No matter what God has called you to do,
You will be tested before He promotes you.**

We must be faithful, obedient, and patient with God's call. God may temporarily lead you to do something. That does not mean the gift is gone or that the calling has disappeared because the gifts and callings of God are without repentance. In other words, God does not change His mind!

According to First Corinthians 12:27, you and I are the Body of Christ and members. Each member has a role to play in the Body.

What is your role? What has God gifted and called you to do?

Whatever God has called you to do, He has also gifted you to do it. You may not have heeded God's call on your life in the past, but that call is still there. The gifts and callings of God are without repentance! Decide today to stir up the gift within you and to accept the call of God. God has called you to be in full-time ministry; maybe He has gifted you with business sense or artistic talent; perhaps you feel especially called to raise a family—whatever God's gifts and callings, determine in your heart right now to be faithful and obedient in carrying out His plan for your life.

Now, no matter how endowed and highly called you are, you need to be thoroughly furnished, if you want to be free from a shipwreck.

Eloquence does not guarantee success,

The degree does not guarantee pedigree,

Beauty does not guarantee marriage,

Anointing does not guarantee ministerial exploits,

Giftedness does not guarantee greatness,

you must acquire all the keys in this book or, you will be **GIFTED BUT STRANDED**

13

2

YOU MUST BE BORN OF THE SPIRIT

The Scriptures speak of the necessity of being "born of the Spirit." Indeed, Jesus said the following in a private meeting with the religious leader Nicodemus.

The truth is, that no one can enter the Kingdom of God without being born of water and the Spirit **(John 3:5 NLT).**

According to Jesus, nobody can enter God's kingdom unless they have been "born of the Spirit." Thus, we must know exactly what that means.

As we look at the Scriptures, we find that there are several things that the Bible says about the subject of being "born of the Spirit." They are as follows.

Being Born of the Spirit Is the New Birth

Being "born of the Spirit" is also referred to as the "new birth." The new birth is the work of the Holy Spirit, which places the believer in a right relationship with the God of the Bible. It is a work of God, not of humans.

John wrote. "Who were born, not of blood nor the will of the flesh nor the will of man, but God" (John 1:13 ESV)

The New Living Translation says:

They are reborn! This is not a physical birth resulting from human passion or plan—this rebirth comes from God (John 1:13 NLT)

The new birth is spiritual. It is something which the Spirit of God performs in our hearts. In other words, we do not give birth to ourselves.

The New Birth Is Necessary for Salvation

The new birth is necessary because all of us are separated from God because of our individual sins. Paul wrote to the Romans.

For all have sinned and come short of the glory of God (Romans 3:23 KJV).

Each of us has fallen short of the perfect standard which God has set. Therefore, none of us can make it to heaven on our merit, our good works.

Furthermore, if a person continues in their sin, there is no hope of salvation for them. Paul also wrote to those in Rome.

For the wages of sin is death (Romans 6:23 KJV).

Death means separation. We are spiritually separated from God at birth. When a person dies apart from Christ, they become eternally separated from Him.

Yet if we trust Jesus Christ as our Savior, salvation is ours. Paul wrote further on this subject to the Romans. He said. "But the gift of God is eternal life in Christ Jesus our Lord (Romans 6:23 NRSV)."

Salvation is a gift that God offers to unbelieving humanity.

Faith Must Be Placed in Jesus Christ for the New Birth

The new birth occurs when faith is placed in the Person of Jesus Christ. In speaking of the nation Israel, John emphasized the necessity of receiving Christ for whom He claimed to be.

But to all who did receive him, who believed in his name, he gave the right to become children of God (John 1:12 ESV).

We become His children when we trust Him as our Savior.

This regenerating work of the Holy Spirit is necessary for everyone. Indeed, there are no exceptions. Paul wrote to Titus.

He saved us, not because of the good things we did, but because of his mercy. He washed away our sins and gave us a new life through the Holy Spirit (Titus 3:5 NLT).

To be saved, one must put his or her faith in Jesus Christ. This is the only way one can have a relationship with the living God.

The Definition of a Christian

The definition of a Christian is a person in whom the Holy Spirit dwells. The Apostle Paul made this clear when he wrote to the church in Rome.

You, however, are not in the flesh but the Spirit, if in fact, the Spirit of God dwells in you. Anyone who does not have the Spirit of Christ does not belong to him (Romans 8:9 ESV)

Here Paul stresses the fact that without the Holy Spirit we do not have Christ. Indeed, the mark of a Christian is the indwelling Spirit of God.

Jude wrote of people who do not have the Spirit. He defined them in this manner.

It is these worldly people, devoid of the Spirit, who are

causing divisions (Jude 19 NRSV).

Those without the Holy Spirit are non-believers. They are worldly people, lost in sin. They are without hope apart from Christ

The Body of the Christian Becomes the Temple of the Holy Spirit

The body of the Christian is called the temple of the Holy Spirit. Paul explained this when he wrote to the Corinthians.

Or don't you know that your body is the temple of the Holy Spirit, who lives in you and was given to you by God? You do not belong to yourself (1 Corinthians 6:19 NLT).

Since the body of each believer is the temple of the Spirit it is the duty of each Christian to keep the temple set apart for service to God. Paul also wrote.

I appeal to you, therefore, brothers and sisters, by the mercies of God, to present your bodies as a living sacrifice, holy and acceptable to God, which is your spiritual worship (Romans 12:1 NRSV).

Our bodies belong to Him; we are no longer our own.

In sum, there are several important things we learn from Scripture about what it means to be "born of the Spirit."

Thus: The Bible says that human beings must be "born of the Spirit" if they want to know the true God and reach heaven. This is not optional. Rather it is necessary and required.

We learn several things about "being born of the Spirit" from Scripture.

First, each of us needs a spiritual rebirth before we can enter the kingdom of heaven. Jesus called it being "born again." As we have each been born physically, we also need to be born spiritually.

The reason we need this spiritual rebirth is that none of us can get to heaven based on our good deeds. Indeed, our sin has separated us from the God of the Bible. Thus, no matter how good we may be, we will never be "good enough."

The new birth consists in believing in Jesus Christ as Savior. Faith must be placed in Him and Him alone. When we do this, we become "born again." At the time of the new birth, the Holy Spirit comes to dwell with us. He not only showed us our need for Christ He also indwells us when we trust Jesus as our Savior. The Spirit of God remains with us during our entire life.

Consequently, there are two types of people in this world. On the one hand, some know Christ and on the other hand, some do not. Christians have the Spirit of God dwelling in them while unbelievers do not.

Finally, the Holy Spirit works in the life of the "born again" Christian to make them more "Christlike." We now belong to Him, and the Spirit of God helps us act like Him. This is a process which continues as long as we are alive.

This is what will guarantee your achievements, massive attainments, and uncommon accomplishments.

Born again, therefore, is a panacea to an escape from a life of being gifted but stranded.

3

THE FRUITS OF THE SPIRIT

The Fruit of the Holy Spirit is a biblical term that sums up nine attributes of a person or community living in accordance with the Holy Spirit. According to

Galatians 5: ***"But the fruit of the Spirit is love, joy, peace, patience, kindness, goodness, faithfulness, gentleness, and self-control.***"[2] The fruit is contrasted with the works of the flesh which immediately precede it in this chapter.

The original Greek term translated as "fruit" is singular. Aquinas explained, "Consequently fruit is mentioned there in the singular, on account of its being generically one, though divided into many species which are spoken of as so many fruits." Augustine's commentary on Galatians 5:25-26 says, "the Apostle had no intention of teaching us how many [either of the flesh, or fruits of the Spirit] there are; but to show how the former should be avoided, and the latter sought after." Let's look at them humbly

Love (Greek: agape, Latin: Caritas)

Agape (love) denotes an undefeatable benevolence and unconquerable goodwill that always seeks the highest good for others, no matter their behavior. It is a love that gives freely without asking anything in return and does not consider the worth of its object. Agape is more a love by choice than phallos, which is love by chance; and it refers to the will rather than the emotion. Agape describes the unconditional love God has for the world. Paul describes love in 1 Corinthians 13:4–8: Saying: Love is patient, love is kind. It does not envy, it does not boast, it is not proud. It does not dishonor others, it is not self-seeking, it is not easily angered, and it keeps no record of wrongs. Love does not delight in evil but rejoices with the truth. It always protects, always trusts, always, and always perseveres. Love never fails. But where there are prophecies, they will cease; where there are tongues, they will be stilled; where there is knowledge, it will pass away.

According to Strong's Greek Lexicon, the word ἀγάπη (Transliteration: agapē) means love, i.e. affection or benevolence; especially (plural) a love feast:—(feast of)

charity, dear, love, affection, goodwill, love, benevolence, brotherly love, love feasts.

The Greek word ἀγάπη (agapē) occurs 117 times in 106 verses in the Greek concordance of the NASB.

Joy (Greek: chara, Latin: Gaudium)

The joy referred to here is deeper than mere happiness; it is rooted in God and comes from Him. Since it comes from God, it is more serene and stable than worldly happiness, which is merely emotional and lasts only for a time.

According to Strong's Greek Lexicon, the Greek word listed in the verse is χαρά meaning 'joy', 'gladness', or a source of joy'. The Greek χαρά (chara) occurs 59 times in 57 verses in the Greek concordance of the NASB.

"joy, delight" (akin to chairs, "to rejoice"), is found frequently in Matthew and Luke, and especially in John, once in Mark (Mark 4:16, RV, "joy," AV, "gladness"); it is absent from 1 Corinthians.

Peace (Greek: Eirene, Latin: pax, Hebrew: Shalom)

The Greek word εἰρήνη (eirēnē) means peace (literally or figuratively); by implication, prosperity:—one, peace, quietness, rest.

The word "peace" comes from the Greek word Eirene, the Greek equivalent of the Hebrew word shalom, which expresses the idea of wholeness, completeness, or tranquility in the soul that is unaffected by the outward circumstances or pressures. The word eirene strongly suggests the rule of order in place of chaos

The Greek εἰρήνη (eirēnē) occurs 92 times in 86 verses in the Greek concordance of the KJV. It also means a state of national tranquility, exemption from the rage and havoc off our peace between individuals, i.e. harmony, concord, security, safety, prosperity, felicity, (because peace and harmony make and keep things safe and prosperous) of the Messiah's peace the way that leads to peace (salvation) of Christianity, the tranquil state of a soul assured of its salvation through Christ, and so fearing nothing from God and content with its earthly lot, of whatsoever sort that is the blessed state of devout and upright men after death.

Jesus is described as the Prince of Peace, who brings peace to the hearts of those who desire it. He says in John 14:27: "Peace I leave with you, My peace I give to you; not as the world gives do I give to you. Let not your heart be troubled, neither let it be afraid". In Matthew 5:9 he says, "Blessed are the peacemakers, for they will be called sons of God."[15]

Patience (Greek: makrothumia, Latin: longanimity)

Generally, the Greek world applied this word to a man who could avenge himself but did not. This word is often used in the Greek Scriptures about God and God's attitude to humans. Exodus 34:6 describes the Lord as "slow to anger and rich in kindness and fidelity."

Patience, which in some translations is "longsuffering" or "endurance", is defined in Strong by two Greek words, **makrothumia** and **hupomone**.

The first, pronounced (mak-roth-oo-mee-ah) comes from macros, "long", and thumos, "temper". The word denotes lenience, forbearance, fortitude, patient endurance, and longsuffering. Also included in makrothumia is the ability to endure persecution and ill-treatment. It describes a person who has the power to exercise revenge but instead exercises restraint.

The latter, hupomone, (hoop-om-on-ay) is translated as "endurance": Constancy, perseverance, continuance, bearing up, steadfastness, holding out, and patient endurance. The word combines hupo, "under", and mone, "to remain". It describes the capacity to continue to bear up under difficult circumstances, not with a passive complacency, but with a hopeful fortitude that actively resists weariness and defeat, with hupomone (Greek ὑπομονή) being further understood as that which would be "as opposed to cowardice or despondency".

"With lowliness and meekness, with longsuffering, forbearing one another in love".

Kindness (Grerestoresotes,)

In Greek, old wine was called "Christos" which meant that it was mellow or smooth. As Christ used this word in Matthew 11:30, "For my yoke is easy, and my burden light."

Kindness is acting for the good of people regardless of what they do, properly, "useable, i.e. well-fit for use (for what is needed); kindness that is also serviceable".

Kindness is goodness in action, the sweetness of disposition, gentleness in dealing with others, benevolence, kindness, and affability. The word describes the ability to act for the welfare of those taxing your patience. The Holy Spirit removes abrasive qualities from the character of one under His control.

The word kindness comes from the Greek word restores (khray-stot-ace), which meant to show kindness or to be friendly to others and often depicted rulers, governors, or people who were kind, mild, and benevolent to their subjects. Anyone who demonstrated this quality of restores was considered to be compassionate, considerate, sympathetic, kind, or gentle. The apostle

Paul uses this word to depict God's incomprehensible kindness for unsaved people (see Romans 11:22; Ephesians 2:7; Titus 3:4

One scholar has noted that when the word restores is applied to interpersonal relationships, it conveys the idea of being adaptable to others. Rather than harshly require everyone else to adapt to his own needs and desires, when restores are working as a believer, he seeks to become adaptable to the needs of those who are around him. (Sparkling Gems from the Greek, Rick Renner)

Kindness is doing something and not expecting anything in return. Kindness is respect and helping others without waiting for someone to help one back. It implies kindness no matter what. We should live "in purity, understanding, patience and kindness; in the Holy Spirit and sincere love; in truthful speech and the power of God; with weapons of righteousness in the right hand and the left".

Goodness (Greek: agathosune, Latin: bonnatiwr)

The state or quality of being good, Moral excellence; virtue;

Kindly feel, kindness, generosity, and joy in being good

The best part of anything is; Essence; Strength;

The general character is recognized in quality or conduct.

Popular English Bibles (e.g. NIV, NASB, NLT) translate the single Greek word restores into two English words: kindness and goodness. "Wherefore also we pray always for you, that our God would count you worthy of this calling, and all the good pleasure of his goodness, and the work of faith with power". "For the fruit of the Spirit is in all goodness and righteousness and truth", with agathosune being "found only in Biblical and ecclesiastical writings, uprightness of heart and life".

Faithfulness (Greek: pistis, Latin: fides)

The root of pistis ("faith") is peithô, that is to persuade or be persuaded, which supplies the core meaning of faith as being "divine persuasion", received from God, and never generated by man. It is defined as the following: objectively, trustworthy; subjectively, trustful:—believe(-ing, -r), faithful(-ly), sure, true.

The Greek πιστός (pistos) occurs 67 times in 62 verses in the Greek concordance of the KJV: faithful (53x), believe (6x), believing (2x), true (2x), faithfully (1x), believer (1x), sure (1x).

trusty, faithful of persons who show themselves faithful in the transaction of business, the execution of commands, or the discharge of official duties

One who kept his plighted faith, worthy of the trust that can be relied on, easily persuaded, believing, confiding, trusting. In the New Testaments writings, one who trusts in God's promises, one who is convinced that Jesus has been raised from the dead. One who has become convinced that Jesus is the Messiah and author of salvation.

Examples:

"O Lord, thou art my God; I will exalt thee, I will praise thy name; for thou hast done wonderful things; thy counsels of old are faithfulness and truth". "I pray that out of his glorious riches he may strengthen you with power through his Spirit in your inner being, so that Christ may dwell in your hearts through faith". Ephesian 3:16-17

The writer of the Letter to the Hebrews describes it this way: "Let us fix our eyes on Jesus, the author and perfecter of our faith, who for the joy set before him endured the cross, scorning its shame, and sat down at the right hand of the throne of God".

Gentleness (Greek: practice, Latin: modestia)

Gentleness, in the Greek, practice, commonly known as meekness, is "a divinely-balanced virtue that can only operate through faith (cf. [1 Timothy 6:11]; [2 Timothy 2:22-25]).[32]

The New Spirit-Filled Life Bible defines gentleness as

"a disposition that is even-tempered, tranquil, balanced in spirit, unpretentious, and that has the passions under control. The word is best translated as 'meekness,' not as an indication of weakness, but of power and strength under control. The person who possesses this quality pardons injuries corrects faults and rules his spirit well".

"Brothers and sisters, if someone is caught in a sin, you who live by the Spirit should restore that person gently. But watch yourselves, or you also may be tempted". [Galatians 6:1]

"Be completely humble and gentle; be patient, bearing with one another in love". [Ephesians 4:2]

Self-control (Greek: enkrateia, Latin: continent)

The Greek word used in Galatians 5:23 is "enkrateia", meaning "strong, having mastery, able to control one's thoughts and actions."

We read also: "...make every effort to add to your faith goodness; and to goodness, knowledge; and to knowledge, self-control; and to self-control, perseverance; and to perseverance, godliness; and to godliness, mutual affection; and to mutual affection, love". [2 Peter 1:5-7]

31

4

FAITH, THE HIGHWAY TO UNUSUAL BREAKTHROUGH

Now faith is the substance of things hoped for, the evidence of things not seen. By it, the elders obtained a good report

Hebrews 11:1-2

 God wants us to rise in faith to see breakthroughs. He is the one who will break through for you, but He needs your cooperation to open the gates - the opening to those closed places - that lie before you faith will do for us so much more!

"It opens the gate of heaven. When heaven's gates open, what is in heaven comes down to earth. Health, wholeness, peace, love, grace, glory, revelation, strategy, and all the rest of the nature of God and His

Kingdom come down when the gates open."

As I have already said, the enemy tries to restrict us. He coils around us and tightens His grip like the python snake. He wants to restrict the Church worldwide, but we know that the Gates of Hades will not prevail against her (Matthew 16:18). Gates are authorized systems of access; gates are exit and entry points that must be opened. Especially when we are at the place threshold, the enemy will try to terminate our forward movement. He will attack with fear and through squeezing the life out of us.

There is warfare at the gates and especially at the threshold of a breakthrough. This is where we must overcome. The Hebrew root meaning for threshold, gate or door is "caphaph" and means "to snatch away or terminate". The other word for threshold is "pethen" which means "to twist like a snake". It even sounds like the python and maybe where the name of this snake originated.

When we are experiencing strong enemy warfare at the gates, it may seem that there is no life or direction but only darkness, despair, and the feeling of being lost. This is not what God wants for us. This is an enemy attack at the point of threshold and breakthrough. He tries to snatch away our destiny and seeks to terminate our work for God at this point. There is fear at the brink or threshold because we are moving into a new place or territory. It is as if we are at the precipice of a mountain and there is a fear of risk because there is a need for more faith to leap over to the other side.

Have you been there? You know you must jump but your flesh does not want to. It's too risky. You might fall.

I made a move to become a Christian, so I would experience this first-hand. I knew I had to jump and make the move, yet it was so hard personally. My cozy home seemed just too comfortable, and the unknown was not very appealing. But after I made that jump and settled into the new place, everything changed, today we are kings by the grace of God

God began to open new doors of breakthrough, but I had to take that first step and by faith go through the gate God had put before me. I won a victory at that gate, but it was a place of real personal battle until I finally stepped through it. I had to wrestle through to a new place of victory. I had to give up what I had before and cross over into that new place (Christ) It wasn't easy, but it was necessary.

We are all overcomers through Christ. He is the one who will win the victory, but we must exercise our faith. He is the one who will break through for us, but He wants our cooperation. We need God's supernatural intervention to break through the gates. Humans can't do it, but God will go before us and breakthrough. He will break through those impenetrable gates before you to bring you into new places of victory.

Isaiah 45:2, "*I will go before you and make the crooked places straight; I will break in pieces the gates of bronze (brass) and cut the bars of iron.*"

I encourage you to persevere in faith, and not give up.

There are breakthroughs in prayer that are close at hand. The enemy is trying to terminate your forward movement. You may be battling in faith and feel hindered by the enemy. Press on and press through for the breaker, Jesus will surely come, and He will come with His resurrection power. Intercessors is key to the harvest that we are beginning to experience in the nations. The enemy knows this and is trying to hinder the prayer movement. He will do this by trying to hinder the faith of God's people. God has been preparing you for the future. This is the time to crossover to a new place and to take new territory for the Kingdom of God. But this involves letting go and moving forward with God in a dimension you have never known before.

Heb 12:1 NIV. Says: *Therefore, since we are surrounded by such a great cloud of witnesses, let us throw off everything that hinders and the sin that so easily*

entangles. And let us run with perseverance the race marked out for us,

"Crossing over requires us to give up something precious to us such as sin, pleasure, a prized possession. It may be a thing, an attitude, a person, security, or our desire for the future. It can be anything that we hold on to when the only way to get to the other side is to let go of it. There is an aspect of idolatry to that. It has become a god to us, something we worship and to which we are bowing our knees. To cross over will mean to let go of that which will not fit through the gate with us." But, there is a higher calling for glory and honor. Thus: faith becomes necessary if we must not be stranded

5

YIELD ALL CONTORL TO GOD

***Trust in the LORD with all your heart and lean not on your understanding; in all your ways submit to him, and he will make your paths straight.* Proverbs 3:5,6**

Many of you may be at the door, at the threshold point of breakthrough in faith, and the enemy is taunting and trying to stop you from forwarding movement.

The key to our breakthrough is God. What do you need to do to see the breakthrough and touch the God of the breakthrough? Remember, there are things you must let go of to see the breakthrough. Here are some keys that will help release your faith and unlock the door to a breakthrough:

Realize that God is going to break through for you - You can't do it by yourself. He has the resurrection power to break through every obstacle in your life. Meditate on God and His Word until you know that He is the breakthrough God for you.

Yield all control to God - Let go of the known and trust God with the unknown, which will give you access to the other side. So often we try to control our own lives. We must let go of anything that God may want us to give up. We need to yield our will and move to a new level of trust in God.

Wait on God and find out what action He wants you to take - Be still and make sure you know God's leading and guiding your life. Some of you may be in a place of waiting, and it takes faith to wait. But others of you may know what God wants you to do, but you have been hesitant and fearful. Hesitate no longer.

Move forward in faith and obedience - Bold action will open the gate and release God's spiritual power. Do not waver because of fear. Take a leap of faith. God will catch you in His arms on the other side.

Realize that if you refuse to leap at the point of breakthrough, you have chosen to stop. Then you are stuck at that place until you go back and again choose to step out by faith. God will then open new revelation to you. You will wonder why you had succumbed to the spirit of hesitancy. The Bible says in **Hebrews 11:6**, "*And without faith, it is impossible to please God because anyone who comes to him must believe that he exists*

and that he rewards those who earnestly seek him."

We will come to this choice of breakthrough again and again in our lives. God expects us to walk by faith daily. Remember that Jesus' death and resurrection were the greatest places of breakthrough.

Jesus broke through every power of darkness when He died on the cross. His resurrection is the key to all power and all victory against the enemy attacks we face today. We can walk in great faith without fear because our King has already won the battle at the cross. We can pray great prayers without doubt or fear because we pray them in His most powerful Name.

6

INCREASE YOUR CAPACITY

1 Kings 4:29-34 And *God gave Solomon wisdom and understanding exceeding much, and largeness of heart, even as the sand that is on the seashore.*

And Solomon's wisdom excelled the wisdom of all the children of the east country, and all the wisdom of Egypt.

For he was wiser than all men; than Ethan the Ezrahite, and Heman and Darda, the sons of Mahol: and his fame was in all nations roundabout.

And he spake three thousand proverbs: and his songs were a thousand and five.

And he spake of trees, from the cedar tree that is in Lebanon even unto the hyssop that springeth out of the wall: he spake also of beasts, and of fowl, and creeping things, and fishes.

And there came of all people to hear the wisdom of Solomon, from all kings of the earth, which had heard of his wisdom.

Before the enthronement of Solomon, not much was expected of ancient kings. They were only required to govern, handle state affairs, and the ability to win wars. Solomon however redefined kingship in his time by increasing his capacity.

The scripture above tells us that, among many things King Solomon was a:

- Horticulturist

- Botanist

- Poet

- Marine Engineer

- Animal biologist

- Creative artist

- Dramatic artist

In his time, King Solomon wrote 3,000 proverbs and 1,500 songs. The scripture specifically says: *"he had the largeness of heart"* This was not a description of the natural heart of King Solomon; it is also not a description of the state of his emotions; neither is the largeness of heart a physical condition.

This term was indicative of a heart that had reached new boundaries of achievements through God.

The NIV translation describes **"largeness of heart"** differently. It calls it

"a breadth of understanding as measureless as the sand on the seashore"

Solomon's life was reflective of the truth in **Philippians 3:13** says. **"I can do all things through Christ who strengthens me"**

Today many of us are underperforming. We are not increasing our capacity and are thus operating below our full potential. Our failure to increase our capacity is an indication of our underachievement. In the body of Christ today, there is a reckless abandonment of little performances, little results, little achievements, little visions, little godly ambitions, and breakthroughs.

Some years ago, when there was a corporate, local, or national event, it was viewed that pastors were only good enough to say the opening prayer and closing prayers.

However, these are the days when pastors should keep increasing their capacity to be multi-disciplined. In these last days, Christian leaders will preach, heal the sick, and open Banks, schools, universities, airlines and so much more.

But this can only happen when you take responsibility to increase your capacity.

WHAT IS CAPACITY?

Capacity means, Specific ability of an entity (person or organization) or resource measured in quantity and level of quality over an extended period.

Capacity is the ability to receive or contain.

It is the maximum amount, number or quantity that can be received or contained.

Your capacity is an indication of what you can receive, carry, hold, or absorb. It is a measure of ability, a measure of performance.

Your capacity reflects your innate potential for growth, development, or accomplishments. Other words which reflect capacity are measure, resourcefulness, dexterity, aptitude, and skillfulness.

INCREASING YOUR CAPACITY IS, THEREFORE:

* Being able to do things you couldn't do before. It means being able to handle things you previously would not attempt. If you consciously decide to expand your capacity, you will become a different person in the future. You will look back and see how much you've grown.

* Taking it beyond the ability to receive or contain and making it greater in number, size, strength, or quality.

* To augment your gift to become greater in the things you are called to do.

* Accepting the fact that better is not good enough.

* The ability to perform a given task with the highest intensification and magnification.

The problem with our performance is that what we are doing today is a fraction of what God can do to us, in us, with us, through us, and by us. You must accept the fact that yes you can before you can... God himself has no problem with increasing our anointing, finance, influence, and affluence but our capacity is what set the boundaries.

2 Kings 4:1-7 *Now there cried a certain woman of the wives of the sons of the prophets unto Elisha, saying, Thy servant my husband is dead, and thou knowest that thy servant did fear the LORD: and the creditor is*

come to take unto him my two sons to be bondmen.

And Elisha said unto her, what shall I do for thee? Tell me, what hast thou in the house? And she said Thine handmaid hath not anything in the house, save a pot of oil.

Then he said, Go, borrow thee vessels abroad of all thy neighbours, even empty vessels; borrow not a few.

And when thou art come in, thou shalt shut the door upon thee and thy sons, and shalt pour out into all those vessels, and thou shalt set aside that which is full.

So she went from him, and shut the door upon her and upon her sons, who brought the vessels to her; and she poured out.

And it came to pass, when the vessels were full, that she said unto her son, Bring me yet a vessel. And he said unto her, there is not a vessel more. And the oil stayed.

Then she came and told the man of God. And he said, Go, sell the oil, and pay thy debt, and live thou and thy children of the rest.

From the scripture above we hear of a woman that missed an opportunity to become an oil exporter par excellence, but she borrowed a few vessels defying his instructions. "Borrow not a few"

The problem with your status is not in the supply or supplier but the problem is with your reception. The woman had limited containers, so the supply was seized. God never runs out of resources to supply, but the problem is with the man that sets the limit to what God can provide.

8 Tips to increasing your capacity

One year from now, I don't want to be the same person as I am today. I want to grow. I want to become better and better; I want to experience 1,000 times more.

One way to do that, I realize, is by expanding my capacity. Expanding my capacity means being able to do things I was not capable of doing before. It means being able to handle things I previously could not nor would not attempt to do. If you consciously decide to expand your capacity, you will become a different person in the future. You will look back and see how much you have grown.

<u>Here are the eight tips to expand your capacity:</u>

1. Take a new challenge

Expanding your capacity is like weightlifting. If you can lift 100 pounds but keep lifting that all the time, your capacity will not increase. You need to move to the next level and lift something heavier. It will feel difficult at first, but over time it will become easy. Then, once you become comfortable with it, you should lift something even heavier.

Similarly, to expand your capacity you must take on new challenges beyond your comfort zone. Work on something you are not comfortable doing.

Look at your current situation. How long have you been doing what you're doing? When was the last time you limped into a new challenge? If you find yourself in a comfort zone, then shake things up. Find a new challenge and take it.

In my case, I realize that I did not take on a new challenge in the last year or two. I lifted the same weight for far too long. Now that I learn the importance of expanding my capacity, I am working on a new challenge, and I encourage you to expand your reach. Fly higher.

2. Make sure it's exciting

When you are looking for a challenge to take, make sure that it is something you are excited about. I have tried to work on a challenge I was not excited about. The results were wasted time, money, and effort. Working on something thatmis not exciting feels like a chore. I must push myself to do it.

On the other hand, if I work on something exciting then working on it feels effortless. Sure, there are times when I need to motivate myself, but the total amount of energy needed to get things going is much, much lower. Furthermore, I enjoy the time working on it. I want more, not less. As a result, I move further quickly and achieved.

3. Make it fun

Not only should you take on an exciting challenge, but also you should make the process fun. In my case, I like to think of a challenge as a game. I have the challenge to overcome, and I have some resources at hand. I need to allocate my resources wisely and work my way over the obstacles. There are surprises and pitfalls along the way. It is like a game? Enjoy the opportunity to learn something new.

Thinking of a challenge as a game makes me more excited about it. It also makes it easier to handle failure. After all, losses are as normal as winning in sports. Both results are designed to teach me something. A learner has a willingness to loss to gain knowledge. If I want to become a better player, I must have a willingness to loss to learn. Rather than the lost discouraging me, they make me even more motivated to increase my skills. So, I can rise to challenge the challengers again. Until I have mastered my skills.

4. Focus

If the challenge is beyond your comfort zone, as it should be, then it will not be easy. You need to focus your heart and mind on it. Do not spread yourself too thin. Do not try to do too many things at once. That is a recipe for failure.

5. Invest

Some people are willing to take on a new challenge but hesitant to invest their time and money. But if it is a worthy challenge then it is worth your time and money. There is no reason not to invest in it.

Remember the game metaphor above? The resources you have in a game are there to help you achieve the game's objective. You should invest them in weapons, buildings and whatever other tools you need to achieve the objective. Similarly, you should invest your resources to expand your capacity. Do not do it above your mean, of course, hopefully you understand the point.

6. Take risks

The more you know about something, the less the risks

involved. But in the beginning, when you are working on something new, risks are inevitable. Do not be afraid to take them. Those who are not willing to take risks may never move to the level. You might fail but you will learn a lot. They will make you a player.

Who Just safe will regret all the opportunities they have wasted in life. I do not want to be that kind of person. I might fail, but at least I will not have regret because I did not try.

7. Build the desire to "kill"

Your progress will be faster if the desire to "kill" your "enemy", which in this case is the challenge you take. This desire will fuel your effort every day to get better at what you do. It will also make you more resilient in the face of difficulties and failures. Without such a desire, your progress will be slow.

8. Move on

Once you achieve certain level of mastery in a particular challenge, move on and take a new more difficult challenge. Do not stop and be comfortable with where you are. Keep expanding your capacity.

<u>7 Ways to Increase Your Capacity</u>

In **Ecclesiastes 5:18-20** in the Message Bible which says:

"After looking at the way things are on this earth, here's what I've decided is the best way to live: Take care of yourself, have a good time, and make the most of whatever job you have for as long as God gives you life. And that's about it. That's the human lot. Yes, we should make the most of what God gives, both the bounty and the capacity to enjoy it, accepting what's given and delighting in the work. It's God's gift! God deals out joy in the present, the now. It's useless to brood over how long we might live."

As I've read and re-read that verse in preparing and putting this book together, . . . I was stirred by **Ecclesiastes 5:19** which say:

"Yes, we should make the most of what God gives both the bounty and the capacity to enjoy it."

The word capacity ignited in my spirit and God showed me seven ways to expand our capacity for as we move in His blessing flow.

But first, let's lay a foundation for this chapter. I've read **Isaiah 54** many times . . . generally focusing on **verse 17** particularly in the Amplified Bible which says:

"But no weapon that is formed against you shall prosper, and every tongue that shall rise against you in judgment you shall show to be in the wrong. This

[peace, righteousness, security, triumph over opposition] is the heritage of the servants of the Lord [those in whom the ideal Servant of the Lord is reproduced]; this is the righteousness or the vindication which they obtain from me [this is that which I impart to them as their justification], says the Lord."

But on this occasion, I was led to **Isaiah 54:2** which say:

"Enlarge the place of thy tent and let them stretch forth the curtains of thine habitations: spare not, lengthen thy cords, and strengthen thy stakes."

According to Strong's Concordance and the Hebrew dictionary the word enlarge means to:

"grow large, to go beyond, to make more room, to increase capacity, to break out; to breakthrough; to expand, go further, occupy new territories, no limits, no boundaries, thinking big."

Enlarging our tent. . Our reach . . . our capacity for breakthrough is not optional or a suggestion . . . it is a scriptural command for unusual breakthrough.

Each of us knows that when we obey God . . . amazing opportunities and blessings open to us.

As we reflect on where we are in life . . . and what we feel led to do and accomplish we need to believe God to enlarge and expand our horizons. As we walk by faith, we are unleashing a supernatural dynamic where we will experience miraculous breakthroughs by expanding our capacity for His blessing flow. Scripturally speaking I believe we can all agree that God has the ability, the willingness, the desire, and the capacity to bless us superabundantly above all that we could ever think or ask.

However, if we do agree . . . there is a question that needs an answer.

If it is God's desire to bless us by enlarging our borders, then why is it that we are not receiving the blessing flow that God desires for each of us?

I know there is no shortage in heaven . . . that heaven will never run out of the promises and provision promised to the children of God. If there is no shortage of resources in heaven, then the problem lies here on earth . . . with our capacity to receive what heaven releases to each of us. We limit our capacity to receive.

In the story of the widow woman in **2 Kings 4** . . . as soon as her capacity of jars were used up . . . the oil ceased to flow.

2 Kings 4:6 in the Amplified Bible says:

"When the vessels were all full, she said to her son,

bring me another vessel. And he said to her, there is not a one left. Then the oil stopped multiplying."

The oil stopped multiplying when she no longer had the capacity to capture it in the jars.

The woman was able to pay all her debts and save her sons from being taken by her creditors. Not only that, but she received her retirement and that of her sons fully funded in one day. However, if she had more jars . . . . a greater capacity to receive . . . she would have received more and helped her family and neighbors out of debt as well. The lack of jars . . . limited the widow woman's capacity to receive and bless others. When you expand your capacity to give and receive . . . you enlarge your blessing flow. As your capacity increases so does the blessing flow in your life.

Luke 6:38 in the Amplified Bible says:

"Give, and [gifts] will be given to you; good measure, pressed down, shaken together, and running over, will they pour [a]into [the pouch formed by] the bosom [of your robe and used as a bag]. For with the measure you deal out [with the measure you use when you confer benefits on others], it will be measured back to you."

For with the capacity, you deal out . . . with the measure of that capacity you use . . . as you confer benefits on others . . . blessings will be measured back to you.

When our capacity to give is expanded so is our capacity to receive.

The last part of **Luke 6:38** in The Living Bible say:

"Whatever measure you use to give—large or small—will be used to measure what is given back to you"

Our capacity determines our blessing flow. If we can increase our capacity, we can increase our blessing flow.

Psalm 81:10 in The Living Bible says:

"For it was I Jehovah your God who brought you out of the land of Egypt. Only test me! Open your mouth wide and see if I won't fill it. You will receive every blessing you can use!"

As we go through this teaching be mindful of **Isaiah 1:19** in The Living Bible which says:

"If you will only let me help you, if you will only obey, then I will make you rich!"

A closer look at **Isaiah 54:2** reveals five special instructions.

"Enlarge the place of thy tent, and let them stretch forth the curtains of thine habitations: spare not, lengthen thy cords, and strengthen thy stakes;"

Enlarge . . . stretch . . . do not hold back . . . lengthen and strengthen.

In other words, God is telling us to increase our capacity to receive His ever-increasing blessing flow. Our capacity to give and receive determines what we're capable of receiving. God will not result a blessing we cannot handle either spiritually or financially. The children of Israel wandered through the wilderness for 40 years because they did not have the capacity to accept, appreciate and act on the blessings of God. Because of their murmuring . . . only two of the original Israelites who came out of Egypt entered the Promised Land.

A journey that should have taken less than two weeks . . . took forty years. Our capacity to receive and understand the blessing flow of God will either release or limit our potential for 1,000 times more. To increase our capacity, we must learn to take God at His Word and to think beyond our imagination.

But first, we must increase our capacity beyond our current capacity of understanding.

Luke 5:1-2 says*: "And it came to pass, that, as the people pressed upon him to hear the word of God, he stood by the lake of Gennesaret, and saw two ships standing by the lake: but the fishermen were gone out of them, and were washing their nets."*

Let's study **Luke 5:3** for a moment..... *Little from the land. And he sat down, and taught the people out of the ship."*

Have you ever wondered why Jesus taught first...before the miracles took place? Jesus did not tell Peter to cast his nets to the other side, get some fish, have a fish fry and give his fellow fishermen the benefits of the miracle?

Put yourself in Peter's shoes ... he had fished all night long .... He caught nothing ... now the boat is cleaned and he's ready to go to IHOP for the rooty tooty, fresh and fruity breakfast special. If Jesus had walked up and just said, cast your nets out into the deep on the other side of the boat, Peter would have probably said, "Sorry I'm going to eat breakfast then I'm going home to sleep." Peter would have heard Jesus' words, but he would not have understood. The teaching expanded Peter's capacity to believe. Let me say that again, the teaching expanded Peter's capacity to receive. Jesus knew Peter needed to enlarge his thinking . . . to increase His capacity . . . to understand the miracle working power of God.

Luke 5:4-5 says:

"Now when he had left speaking (teaching), he said unto Simon, Launch out into the deep, and let down

your nets for a draught. 5 And Simon answering said unto him, Master, we have toiled all the night, and have taken nothing: nevertheless at thy word I will let down the net. 6 And when they had this done, they enclosed a great multitude of fishes: and their net brake."

Miracle manifestation came into their lives once they understood . . . allowing them to increase their capacity for God's blessing flow of 1,000 times more. Peter might have been skeptical but because of what he heard, he decided to step out into the unknown.

Now here's another question for you...did Jesus make the fish appear?

No, the fish were there all the time. The miracle was always their Peter just had to have his capacity to understand and receive increased.

The fish were there...but Peter had to changed his perception.....He said, *"Master we have toiled all night long....but at your word, we'll let down the net."*

Peter's faith had increased because his capacity to understanding increased.

Here's a fact, what you perceive will become your reality. When we perceive right things . . . our capacity to receive God's blessing flow increases.

As we increase our capacity to understand . . . it allows us to put our nets where the miracles are waiting. Our faith increases our capacity to receive. It's also important to understand that our capacity to receive must be enlarged in the triune man (spirit, soul, and body). We may be spiritually sound . . . with great understanding but God does not want us to ignore our soul and body. Our ability to increase our spiritual capacity is directly proportional to our time reading and studying the Word, praying, worshipping through our voice and our checkbook. Giving, as we've taught before, is an act of worship. God will only increase the spiritual capacity of those who have a hunger for His Word and His presence. Our soul refers to our mind (intellectual capacity) our will (decision making capacity) and our emotions (our capacity for feeling things). God tells us numerous times in scripture that He does not want us ignorant.

1 Corinthians 12:1 says: ***"Now concerning spiritual gifts, brethren, I would not have you ignorant."***

Increasing our body capacity doesn't mean weight gain. It means our health, our relationships and capacity for success.

<u>Here are seven keys to increasing our capacity in spirit, soul and body.</u>

1. ASK GOD TO INCREASE YOUR CAPACITY.

1 Chronicles 4:10 in the Amplified Bible says:

"Jabez cried [prayed] to the God of Israel, saying, oh, that you would bless me and enlarge my border, and that your hand might be with me, and You would keep me from evil so it might not hurt me! And God granted his request."

Have you ever asked God to increase your borders . . . your capacity for a greater blessing flow?

I'd like to believe that most of you have. However, the real question is did you ask in faith believing . . . not wavering or doubting?

I've known way too many believers whose faith comes in sudden bursts when their back is against the wall or even when it's convenient. When we ask God . . . we've got to know that He is a rewarder of them that diligently seek Him.

2. CHARGE OUT OF YOUR COMFORT ZONE BY CHALLENGING THE WAY YOU THINK.

Stretch your thinking . . . increase your understandings . . . do something you've never done . . . enlarge your capacity for increase by believing something . . . you previously thought impossible.

Believe God like Abraham who left what was familiar and held onto the promises of God. Believe God like Noah who had never seen rain but built the ark. Believe God like the Centurion who knew one word from Jesus would bring life to a dead situation. Believe God like David who took a rock and rolled the giant.

If God is going to enlarge your borders, you will need to leave your comfort zone and the predictable behind so He can increase your capacity to believe and receive beyond your previous expectations.

Genesis 12:1-2 in the Amplified Bible says:

"Now [in Haran] the Lord said to Abram, Go for yourself [for your own advantage] away from your country, from your relatives and your father's house, to the land that I will show you.

"2 And I will make of you a great nation, and I will bless you [with abundant increase of favors] and make your name famous and distinguished, and you will be a blessing [dispensing good to others]."

3. PUT ON YOUR SPIRITUAL GLASSES.

We must stop looking at life through our rearview mirror at what's happened or didn't happen in the past. Our future is in front of us, and we need to allow the Word of God to be the glasses through which we view our capacity for success. We need to see the world before us through the promises of the Word.

To increase our capacity for success, our blessing flow of 1,000 we need to have a great vision.

2 Chronicles 20:20 says: *"Jehoshaphat stood and said, Hear me, O Judah, and ye inhabitants of Jerusalem; Believe in the Lord your God, so shall ye be established; believe his prophets, so shall ye prosper."*

To believe the Lord our God is to see things as He sees them. Take a moment to allow that statement to sink in ... He is the God of unusual breakthrough and limitless possibilities.

4. THE MIRACLE OF THINKING BIG .... LIKE GOD.

Years ago, I read a book entitled "The Magic of Thinking Big" by David J. Schwartz. It's a good book but, truthfully, I'm not into magic, I'm into miracles, the supernatural intervention of God to change circumstances. Miracles Come When You Think Big and Don't Doubt. When our thoughts line up with His thoughts and they should because

1 Corinthians 2:16 in the Amplified Bible says:

"For who has known or understood the mind (the counsels and purposes) of the Lord so as to guide and

instruct Him and give Him knowledge? But we have the mind of Christ (the Messiah) and do hold the thoughts (feelings and purposes) of His heart"

Colossians 3:16 in the Amplified Bible says:

"Let the word [spoken by] Christ (the Messiah) have its home [in your hearts and minds] and dwell in you in [all its] richness, as you teach and admonish and train one another in all insight and intelligence and wisdom [in spiritual things, and as you sing] psalms and hymns and spiritual songs, making melody to God with [His] grace in your hearts."

Now that is how we expand our capacity for success and His blessing flow.

5. NEGATIVE CONVERSATIONS WILL ADVERSELY AFFECT OUR CAPACITY FOR INCREASE.

We can never be motivated by those who are not motivated. We can never share dreams with those who are not dreamers. We cannot talk about achieving our goals with those who don't have any. If we desire to increase our capacity, we need to make sure we hang around the folks who can help fill that capacity with the pure, the powerful and the positive from God. People who will cause us to stretch our thinking while expanding our borders.

1 Corinthians 15:33 in the Amplified Bible says:

"Do not be so deceived and misled! Evil companionships (communion, associations) corrupt and deprave good manners and morals and character."

6. Positive associations will dramatically increase our capacity for success.

Make it your business to learn from people who have been or are at where you want to go we call them monitors.

In selecting a mentor here are three things you should consider.

First, does your mentor have the proper spiritual insight to train you?

Second, has your mentor experienced the advice they are giving you?

Third, does your mentor have a successful track record in the area in which they're advising you, be it the marketplace or ministry?

Advice that has not been tested, proven and successful is just opinion, experiment, not experience.

Someone, regardless of how good they sound cannot

take you where they haven't been.

When it comes to your capacity for success and change you need to realize that every new generation can go beyond the previous generation.

Proverbs 15:22 in the New Living Translation says:

"Plans go wrong for lack of advice; many advisers bring success."

7. **No one can limit or restrict your capacity for success unless you allow them to do so.**

Enlarge your tent, the place of your surroundings. Make and take conscious decisions to move beyond past limitations.

According to the Herring Life Experiences Dictionary, breakthrough is defined as:

"A sudden burst of faith that will take you beyond all previous points of past resistance"

In other words, it is you, nobody else but you will make a decision to move beyond the boundaries that societal inertia or attacks of the enemy have taken you.

May your capacity for success be commensurate with the blessing flow that God is bringing into your life beginning today.

Psalm 40:5-7 in the Amplified Bible says:

"5 Many, O Lord my God, are the wonderful works which you have done, and your thoughts toward us; no one can compare with You! If I should declare and speak of them, they are too many to be numbered.

6 Sacrifice and offering you do not desire, nor have You delight in them; You have given me the capacity to hear and obey [Your law, a more valuable service than] burnt offerings and sin offerings [which] You do not require.

7 Then said I, Behold, I come; in the volume of the book it is written of me;"

Read your Bible, do what it says, and these seven words will guide you to your increased capacity.

One final thought.

Your capacity for success is directly affected by your generosity.

2 Corinthians 9:11 in the New Living Translation says:

"Yes, you will be enriched in every way so that you can always be generous. And when we take your gifts to those who need them, they will thank God."

And, one more scripture on increasing your capacity..

2 Corinthians 9:10 in the New Living Translation says:

"For God is the one who provides seed for the farmer and then bread to eat. In the same way, he will provide and increase your resources and then produce a great harvest of generosity in you."

7

MENTORSHIP OPENS DOORS

Mentorship Is The Transference Of Wisdom.

Wisdom is the most powerful force on earth. It is the difference between poverty and prosperity; Decrease and increase; loss and gain. Throughout the Ancient Writings comes the teachings:

"Wisdom is the principal thing..." (**Proverbs 4:7a**).

Here Are 12 Important Facts You

Should Know About Wisdom:

> 1. Wisdom Is The Master Key To Releasing All The Treasures Of Life Contained In God's Promise. Solomon discovered this. In his unforgettable Dream, God spoke,
> *"...Because this was in thine heart, and thou hast not asked riches, wealth, or honour, nor the life of thine enemies, neither yet hast*

asked long life; but hast asked wisdom and knowledge for thyself, that thou mayest judge my people, over whom I have made thee king: Wisdom and knowledge is granted unto thee; and I will give thee riches, and wealth, and honour, such as none of the kings have had that have been before thee, neither shall there any after thee have the like" (**2 Chronicles 1:11,12**).

2. Wisdom Is Not Necessarily Inherited Genetically Through Your Bloodline. A wise father can have a foolish son.

"...A wise son maketh a glad father: but a foolish son is the heaviness of his mother" (**Proverbs 10:1.** See also **Proverbs 10:5.**)

3. All The Treasures Of Wisdom And Knowledge Are Hidden In Jesus Christ.

"That their hearts might be comforted, being knit together in love, and unto all riches of the full assurance of understanding, to the acknowledgment of the mystery of God, and of the Father, and of Christ; In whom are hid all the treasures of wisdom and knowledge" (**Colossians 2:2,3**).

4. Everything you could possibly desire, will come through your obedience and relationship with Jesus Christ!

The Holy Spirit Is The Spirit Of Wisdom That Imparts And Uses Your Gifts, Talents And Skills.

"...every wise hearted man, in whom the Lord put wisdom and understanding to know how to

work all manner of work for the service of the sanctuary, according to all that the Lord had commanded" (**Exodus 36:1**. See also **1 Corinthians 12**.)

5. Wisdom Is More Powerful Than Weapons Of War.
"Wisdom is better than weapons of war..." **(Ecclesiastes 9:18a).**

6. The Mantle Of Wisdom Can Make You Ten Times Stronger Than Those Without It.

"Wisdom strengtheneth the wise more than ten mighty men which are in the city" **(Ecclesiastes 7:19).**

7. Wisdom Makes Your Enemies Helpless Against You.
"For I will give you a mouth and wisdom, which all your adversaries shall not be able to gainsay nor resist" (**Luke 21:15**).

8. Wisdom Creates Currents Of Favour And Recognition Towards You.
"Exalt her, and she shall promote thee: she shall bring thee to honour, when thou dost embrace her" (**Proverbs 4:8**).
One Thousand Times More Wisdom will create One Thousand Times More favour towards your life!

9. Wisdom Guarantees Your Promotion.

"Exalt her, and she shall promote thee: she shall bring thee to honour, when thou dost embrace her. She shall give to thine head an ornament of grace: a crown of glory shall she deliver to thee" **(Proverbs 4:8, 9).**

10. When You Increase Your Wisdom, You Will Increase Your Wealth.
"Riches and honour are with me; yea, durable riches and righteousness" **(Proverbs 8:18).**

11. Your Investment In Books And Tapes Is Proof Of Your Passion For Wisdom. Paul urged Timothy,
"Study to show yourself approved..." **(2 Timothy 2:15a).**

Your willingness to invest in knowledge is a signal that you understand the rewards of wisdom.

12. Wisdom Is Transferred Through Relationships.
"He that walketh with the wise men shall be wise: but a companion of fools shall be destroyed" **(Proverbs 13:20).**
Yes, wisdom can even be imparted by the laying on of hands by a powerful man of God.

"And Joshua the son of Nun was full of the spirit of wisdom; for Moses had laid his hands upon

him: and the children of Israel hearkened unto him..." **(Deuteronomy 34:9).**

Wisdom even affects the willingness of others to listen to you!

There are two ways to receive wisdom throughout your life: Mistakes and Mentors.

Mentors are gifts from God.

Mentors are gates to greatness.

Mentors are bridges to blessings.

Mentors create uncommon increase.

Mentors are more than just teachers. Teachers focus on information while a Mentor focuses on the protégé.

An Uncommon Mentor is more than a cheerleader. He is a coach, showing you how to achieve your goal.

There Are 4 Types of Mentorships:

Parental Mentorship
Is The Wisdom Received Through Your Parents. It is the first proof of humility. It involves the first commandment with a promise that if you honour your mother and father, it will go well with you throughout your lifetime. (Ephesians 6:1-3.)

Pastoral Mentorship

Is The Wisdom Received through Your Spiritual Leader and Pastor of your Church Scriptures commands us to

"Forsake not the assembling of ourselves together... And so much the more, as ye see the day approaching" **(Hebrews 10:25).**

Professional Mentorship

Is The Wisdom You Receive Through Your Employer, Supervisors And Career Stages. **(Read. Ephesians 6:4-8.)**

Prophetic Mentorship

Is Wisdom That Comes Through Uncommon Anointing Of Uncommon Men Of God Assigned To You During Crisis And Critical Turning Points Of Your Life. It may be healing, financial or relationship oriented. But, the Ancient Writings confirm that the secrets of God are hidden inside men and women of God. *"Surely the Lord God will do nothing, but He revealeth His secret unto His servants the prophets"* (Amos 3:7).

"Believe in the Lord your God, so shall ye be establish; believe His prophets, so shall ye prosper" **(2 Chronicles 20:20).**

God reveals information to those who walk in obedience to Him. When you honor their mantle, extraordinary promotion and events occur. One of the most powerful examples I've ever studied was in the life of Saul, son of Kish. Saul discovered this kind of impartation when he and his servant pursued the presence of Samuel, the prophet. Within hours, Saul was anointed for kingship. It happened in a single day. Why? He entered the presence of an uncommon man of God who could see into his future.

Never forget this powerful principle: "The Secret of the Lord is with them that fear Him; and He will shew them His covenant" (Psalm 25:14).

13 Important Facts About Exceptional Mentorship:

Exceptional Mentorship Will Require The Investment Of Time.
Elisha stayed in the presence of Elijah. Ruth persisted in remaining with Naomi even though she had to move into another country. Joshua stayed under the authority of Moses. David always pursued the presence and counsel of Samuel, his prophet and Mentor. The disciples invested time in the presence of Jesus, away from the crowds.

Everything You Know Came Through Mentorship.
When you were a baby, you were taught to walk, eat, and even dress yourself.

Exceptional Mentors Can Create Uncommon Protégés.
Look at the fishermen, Peter, James, and John, who became renown. They simply had an Uncommon Mentor. An Uncommon Mentor can completely erase the scars and defects

created by past prejudices and wounds. Jesus did it for the 12 disciples. The Holy Spirit is doing it for many today.

Exceptional Mentors Require Pursuit.
You always reach for what you truly desire. The prove of desire is in the pursuit. The passion within you will determine your pursuit of your Mentorship.

An exceptional Dream Will Always Require Exceptional Mentorship.
Solomon received a powerful Assignment to build the great temple of Jerusalem. His Mentor. The incredible and unforgettable King David. He even helped him collect the materials necessary for its completion.

Exceptional Mentorship Can Take Place Anywhere.
Jesus taught in synagogues **(Luke 13:10).** Then, He also taught in villages (**Mark 6:6**).

The Exceptional Mentor Will Always Be An Enemy To The Enemy Of His Protégé.
Jesus reflected this when He warned Peter regarding Satan.
". ...Simon, Simon, behold, Satan hath desire to have you, that he may sift you as wheat: But I have prayed for thee, that thy faith fail not: and when thou art converted, strengthen thy brethren" (Luke **22:31, 32**).

The Mentor will fight against any philosophy, pitfalls or

prejudices that would rob the Protégé of experiencing the One Thousand Times More Blessings in his life.

The Exceptional Mentor Knows Precisely The Path The Protégé Must Take To Unleash The Harvest Of furtunes.

That's why Paul advised Timothy to *"Shew himself approved unto God, a workman that needed not to be ashamed."*

The Exceptional Mentor Willingly Risks The Anger And Even The Alienation Of Protégés To Keep Them Qualified To Receive The Increase Of uncommon fortunes.

You see, the focus of the Mentor is the protection of the Protégé, not the love from the Protégé. The Prophet Samuel was swift to correct Saul and David. Why? To prevent their experience of pain.

The Exceptional Mentor Has Something You Do Not Have Because He Knows Something You Do Not Know.

Discoveries determine progress. Discoveries determine relationships.

"Wisdom is the principal thing... Exalt her, and she shall promote thee; she shall bring thee to honour, when thou dost embrace her" (Proverbs 4:7a, 8).

The Exceptional Mentor Measures The Passion Of The Protégé By His Pursuit Of The Mentor.

What you respect, you will attract. You will never possess what you are unwilling to pursue.

The Exceptional Mentor Exposes Fraudulent People To His Protégé.

Jesus exposed the Pharisees to His disciples, *"But all their works they do for to be seen of men: they make broad their phylacteries, and enlarge the borders of their garments,"* (Matthew 23:5).

One of the master keys to unlocking One uncommon furtunes in your life is to detect enemies and thieves of increase in your life. That's one of the powerful benefits of staying close to a proven and Uncommon Mentor.

The Exceptional Mentor Can Often Predict The Potential—Weakness And Pitfall Of A Protégé. Jesus did this for Peter.

"..I tell thee, Peter, the cock shall not crow this day, before that thou shalt thrice deny that thou knowest me" (Luke 22:34).

Now, the Mentor does not withdraw from the Protégé because of it. He becomes an intercessor because of it! (Read **Luke 22:31,32.**)

I am just now learning how to be a protégé after all these years of life and ministry. that may be your testimony. If yes, here are some of the things that you must start learning.

They move toward popularity. They are fashion conscious. They fall into the comparison trap between what their Mentor offers them and someone else offers them. They are obviously "for hire." They will move away from a Mentor the moment there is serious correction, a higher salary offered, or when the Mentor experiences an unexpected disaster. Just like the prodigal son wanted what the father had for his own pleasure, so it is with the Prodigal Protégé.

8

TAKE THE PATH OF OBEDIENCE

Obedience is the only thing God ever requires. It is His obsession. It seems that it's the only thing on His mind. Ever. It is The Master Key to an escape from a life being gifted but stranded.

***"If ye be willing and obedient, ye shall eat the good of the land:"* (Isaiah 1:19).**

I had a life-changing experience many years ago. God began to reveal to me that my only responsibility was 24 hours of obedience. The past was over. The future was not yet born. My only focus should be 24 hours of hourly obedience. Little did I realize that it would launch me into a season of incredible and unexplainable increase in my life. Now, I realize it was the Master Key to a life of glory and honor.

The Holy Spirit talked to me about continuous obedience, hour by hour. Previously, I had laughed at novices in the church that always stated, "God told me this, and God told me that." Sadly, because many unlearned and untaught people confuse their imagination with the Holy Spirit, it has been a neglected principle and truth—God does talk to you more than anyone else on this earth, continuously.

Time Tasted Truths About The Master

Key Of Obedience:

Obedience Is Doing Anything God Commands You To Do, Regardless Of The Cost Or Consequences. Jesus taught it.
"If ye love me, keep my commandments" (John 14:15).

Obedience To The Word Of God Is the Only Duty Of Man.
"Let us hear the conclusion of the whole matter: Fear God and keep his commandments: for this is the whole duty of man. For God shall bring every work into judgement, with every secret thing, whether it be good, or whether it be evil" (Eccl. 12:13, 14)
This is one of the most important scriptures I found in the Bible. And the first I pasted on the wall of my secret place

Your Obedience Is the Only Evidence That You Truly Know God. John taught this key
"And hereby we do know that we know Him, if we keep His commandments" (1 John 2:3)

Obedience Is An Hourly Event on the Path the path of a life of glory and honor. The Apostle Paul wrote,

"For as many as are led by the Spirit of God, they are the sons of God" **(Romans 8: 14)**
"The Lord your

God hath multiplied you.

And behold, ye are this day as the

Stars of heaven for a multitude.

(The Lord God of your fathers makes you a

Thousand times so many more as ye are, and

Bless you, as He hath promised you).

(Deuteronomy 1:10, 11).

Your agenda for today should be decided in the presence of God. Your daily schedule will create miracles or mistakes, tragedies or triumphs depending on whether you are led by the Spirit of God or not Hourly. Your inner peace is a signal. Don't make a telephone call, an appointment, or a decision unless you have peace in your heart about it.

The Instructions Of God Are Never Unreasonable. The Apostle Paul spoke,

"I beseech you therefore, brethren, by the mercies of God, that ye present your bodies a living sacrifice, holy, acceptable unto God, which is your reasonable service" **(Romans 12:1).**

Your Mind Requires Daily Renewing for Daily Obedience To The Continual Instructions Of God. Paul taught this.

"And be not conformed to this world: but be ye transformed by the renewing of your mind, that ye may prove what is that good, and acceptable, and perfect, will of God" **(Romans 12:2).**

That's why I focus each morning on hearing the Scriptures on cassette tape. His Word washes my mind, my thoughts, and the meditation of my heart. It is the greatest success habit on earth. You cannot have a great life until you have a pure life. You cannot have a pure life unless you have a pure mind. You cannot have a pure mind until it is washed with the Word of God daily.

Nothing Offered As A Substitution For Your Obedience Will Be Accepted By God. The Prophet Samuel taught this.

"And Samuel said, hath the Lord as great delight in burnt offerings and sacrifices, as in obeying the voice of the Lord? Behold, to obey is better than sacrifice, and to hearken than the fat of rams" **(1 Samuel 15:22).**

Your Obedience Is The Miracle Magnet That Keeps The Presence Of God Around You.

"Lord, who shall abide in thy tabernacle? Who shall dwell in thy holy hill? He that walketh uprightly, and worketh righteousness, and speaketh the truth in his heart" **(Psalm 15:1, 2).**

Your Obedience To The Laws Of God Will Require Your Personal Knowledge Of The Law Of God.
That's why the Apostle Paul Mentored Timothy in pursuing the wisdom of God ***"Study to shew thyself approved unto God, a workman that needeth not to be ashamed, rightly dividing the Word of truth"*** **(2 Timothy 2:15).**

Your Obedience To His Instruction is The Only Proof Of Your Love For God. Jesus taught this.
"He that hath My commandments, and keepeth them, he it is that loveth Me..." ***(John 14:21a).***
John embraced this principle.

"But whose keepeth His Word, in him verily is the love of God perfected: hereby know we that we are in Him' **(1 John 2:5).**

Disobedience To God Always Produces Devastating Consequences.
"Then shall they call upon me, but I will not answer; they shall seek me early, but they shall not find me: For that they hated knowledge, and did not choose the fear of the Lord: Therefore shall they eat of the fruit of their own way, and be filled with their own device? **(Proverbs 1:28, 29, 31).**
Isaiah warned:

"But if ye refuse and rebel, ye shall be devoured by the sword: for the mouth of the Lord hath spoken it" (Isaiah 1:20).

Your Obedience Guarantees That God Will Always Respond Favorably To Your Requests

"And whatsoever we ask, we receive of Him... Because we keep His commandments, and do those things that are pleasing in His sight" (1 John 3:

The favor of God is the greatest force necessary to produce the harvest of a glorious life

Obedience Is The Proof You Are Truly A Child Of God. Jesus spoke, *"My sheep hear my voice, and I know them, and they follow me:"* (John 10:27).

The Word of God is The Voice Of God You Must Obey. Peter explained it clearly. *"We have also a more sure word of prophecy; whereunto ye do well that ye take heed, as unto a light that shineth in a dark place, until the day dawn, and the day star arise in your hearts: Knowing this first that no prophecy of the Scripture is of any private interpretation. For the prophecy came not in old time by the will of man: but holy men of God spake as they were moved by the Holy Ghost"* (2 Peter 1:19-21).

The Greatest Quality Of Jesus Was His Obedience To The Will Of The Father. Paul wrote,

"But made Himself of no reputation, and took upon Him the form of a servant, and was made in the likeness of men: And being found in fashion as a man, He humbled Himself, and became obedient unto death, even the death of the cross" (Philippians 2:7,8).

Promotion Always Follows Your Obedience.
It happened in the life of Jesus. As Paul wrote,

"And being found in fashion as a man, He humbled Himself, and became obedient unto death, even the death of the cross. Wherefore God also hath highly exalted Him, and given Him a name which is above every name: ..." (Philippians 2:8, 9).

Jesus Considered His Acts Of Obedience To Be An Example For Your Obedience.
"Ye call me Master and Lord: and ye say well; for so I am. If I then, your Lord and Master, have washed your feet; ye also ought to wash one another's feet. For I have given you an example, that ye should do as I have done to you. Verily, verily I say unto you. The servant is not greater than his lord; neither He that is sent greater than He that sent Him (John 13:13-16).

When You Obey An Instruction From God, Joy Will Result And Be The Proof Of His Pleasure In You. (Proverbs 29:18b).

Jesus Guaranteed That He Would Personally Live In The Heart Of Anyone Who Was Obedient.

> *"...lf a man love me, he will keep My Words: and My Father will love him, and we will come unto him, and make our abode with him"* (John 14:23).

Your Obedience Guarantees The Friendship Of God.

> *"Ye are my friends, if ye do whatsoever I command you"* (John 15:14).

Obedience Is The Proof Of Love.

> *"Jesus answered and said unto him, if a man loves me, he will keep My words: and My Father will love him, and We will come unto him, and make Our abode with him. He that loveth me not keepeth not my sayings: and the word which ye hear is not Mine, but the Father's which sent Me"* (John 14:23, 24).

Your Obedience To Any Instruction From God Will Create Remarkable And Indescribable Peace. Jesus promised,

> *"Peace I leave with you, my peace I give unto you: not as the world giveth, give I unto you..."* (John 14:27a). The Apostle Paul wrote,
> *"And let the peace of God rule in your hearts..." (Colossians 3:15a).*

Focusing on God and His Word creates peace of mind. The Prophet Isaiah said, *"Thou wilt keep him in perfect peace, whose mind is stayed on Thee: because he trusteth in Thee"* (Isaiah 26:3).

Obedience Does Not Always Appear Logical To The Natural Mind. *"There is a way which seemeth right unto a man, but the end thereof are the ways of death"* (Proverbs 14:12).

Sometimes what God tells you to do will appear illogical and even ridiculous. It may even deprive you of an immediate gratification. It may wound your pride. Sometimes, an instruction seems totally unrelated to the miracle you are pursuing, but it will always be rewarded.

When Joshua wanted to defeat Jericho, an illogical instruction came. Walk around the walls of Jericho seven days in a row, and then, seven times on Sunday. Jesus instructed a man to wash clay and spittle from his eyes in the pool of Siloam. It was two miles away and seemingly an absurd request. But, the obedience was proof that the blind man believed the instructions of Jesus. Miracles come to the obedient, not the logical.

It Is Not Impossible To Obey God.

"For this is the love of God, that we keep His commandments: and His commandments are not grievous" (1 John 5:3).

Jesus declared clearly, "For My yoke is easy, and my burden is light" (Matthew 11:30).

God Will Never Advance You Beyond Your Last Act Of Disobedience. Joshua discovered this. After their horrifying losses in the battle of Ai, he cried out to God. But, one of his people had defied an instruction from God. Joshua discovered something few understand: Individual Disobedience Can Create Corporate Punishment. Every promotion was paralyzed. God spoke to Joshua,

> *"...Get thee up; wherefore liest thou thus upon thy face? Israel hath sinned, and they have also transgressed my covenant which I commanded them: for they have even taken of the accursed thing, and hath also stolen. Dissembled also, and they have put it even among their own stuff"* **(Joshua 7:10, 11).**
>
> When Joshua made it right with God, penalized the rebel, God resumed the victories and promotion for Joshua and the Israelites.

God Has Personally Guaranteed The Defeat Of Anyone Who Persists In Disobedience.

Your disobedience disappoints the heart of God. It stops the blessing.

"Moreover, all these curses shall come upon thee, and shall pursue thee, and overtake thee, till thou be destroyed; because thou hearkenedst not unto the voice of the Lord thy God, to keep His commandments and his status which he commanded thee" **(Deut. 28:45)**

God is always against sin because sin has always destroyed what He loves the most, you and me. Sin is heartache to God. Confront it. Uproot it. Ask His forgiveness. Do it now, even while you are reading these words.

Your Obedience Is Rewarded With Supernatural Protection. God promised this to Israel.

"But if thou shalt indeed obey His voice, and do all that I speak; then I will be an enemy unto thine enemies, and an adversary unto thine adversaries" **(Exodus 23:22).**

Satan will make every attempt to destroy you. Job illustrates this in the great scenario of sorrow and restoration in his life. You are not capable of protecting yourself. Those who love you are incapable of protecting you from every adversary and satanic assault. But, God has guaranteed your protection as a reward for your personal obedience to His laws and principles.

Your Obedience Is The Proof You Trust The Promises Of God To You. God longs to be believed.

"But without faith it is impossible to please Him: for he that cometh to God must believe that He is, and that He is a rewarded of them that diligently seek Him" **(Hebrews 11:6).**

Exceptional Obedience Always Creates Exceptional Miracles. Abraham is a marvellous example. Sarah was too old to produce a child. But Abraham believed God. *"Through faith also Sarah herself received strength to conceive Seed, and was delivered of a child when she* *was past age, because she judged Him faithful who had promised"* (Hebrews 11:11. See Also Romans 4:18-21.)

The Disobedience Of One Person Can Cause Tragedies For Thousands.

It happened when Achan sinned and kept the accursed thing, under the leadership of Joshua. (See **Joshua chapter 7.**) When Korah rebelled against the leadership of Moses, hundreds were destroyed because of it. (See **Numbers chapter 16.**) Adam introduced sorrow into the human race. Paul writes,

"For as by one man's disobedience many were made sinners..." (Romans 5:19a).

The Obedience Of One Person Can Bring Awesome Miracles To Thousands. When Moses embraced the leadership of Israel in total obedience to God, millions were delivered. When David accepted the challenge of Goliath, the Israelites went free. When Peter preached obediently on the day of Pentecost, thousands received and believed the message of Jesus. When the Apostle Paul surrendered obediently to the call of God, he rewrote the history of the church.

Your Obedience To Tithe Faithfully Opens The Windows Of Heaven And Guarantees Supernatural Provision For Your Family. Malachi declares,

"Bring ye all the tithes into the storehouse, that there may be meat in Mine house. and prove Me now herewith, saith the Lord of hosts, if I will not open you the windows of heaven and pour you out a blessing,

that there shall be no room enough to receive it, And I will rebuke the devourer for your sakes, and he shall not destroy the fruits of your ground; neither shall your vine cast her fruit before the time of the lie saith the Lord of hosts" **(Malachi 3:10, 11).**

Your Obedience To Confront Strife Will Create Peace.

"Cast out the scorner; and contention shall go out; yea, strife and reproach shall cease" **(Proverbs 22:10).**

 Always mark contentious people. Do not give them an opportunity to poison your world. Take charge. Confront it. An answer comes and solutions will emerge.

Your Obedience To Hear The Word Of God In Your Life Will Birth Great Faith Within You.

"So then faith cometh by hearing, and hearing by the Word of God" **(Romans 10:17).**

Someone said, "Faith comes when you hear God talk." What you read will affect what you believe. Feeding Scriptures into your heart causes faith to come alive. Faith is confidence in God. When you hear anything God is saying, faith will come alive in your heart. What you keep hearing, you eventually believe.

Your Obedience To Forgive Others Guarantees that God Will Forgive You.

"For if ye forgive men their trespasses, your heavenly Father will also forgive you: But if ye forgive not men their trespasses, neither will your Father forgive your trespasses" **(Matthew 6:14, 15).**

Your Obedience To Give Alms To The Unfortunate Guarantees Public Blessing From The Father.

"That thine alms may be in secret: and thy Father which seeth in secret Himself shall reward thee openly" **(Matthew 6:4).**

Your Obedience To Show Mercy And Forgiveness To Others Guarantees that Mercy And Forgiveness Will Return To You From Others.

"Give, and it shall be given unto you; good measure, pressed down, and shaken together, and running over, shall men give into your bosom. For with the same measure that ye mete withal it shall be measured to you again" **(Luke 6:38).**

Disobedience Will Always Bring The Chastening Of The Lord.

"For whom the Lord loveth, He chasteneth, and scourgeth every son whom He receiveth. Now no chastening for the present seemeth to be joyous, but grievous: nevertheless afterward it yieldeth the peaceable fruit of righteousness unto them which are exercised thereby" **(Hebrews 12:6, 11).**

Endure correction. Wisdom begins with correction. Errors must be exposed. Mistakes must be faced. The person who corrected you the most is possibly the person you love the most. Hell is filled of people who rejected correction. Heaven is filled of people who accepted it.

Your Obedience To Pursue Wise Counsel Will Always Be Rewarded With Safety.

"Where no counsel is, the people fall: but in the multitude of counsellors there is safety" (**Proverbs 11:14**)

Ignorance is deadly. Don't risk it. Listen to godly Mentors. Somebody knows something that will help you survive and even succeed during the most in painful seasons of your life.

Your Obedience To Parental Authority Guarantees Uncommon Blessing For A Lifetime.

"Children, obey your parents in the Lord: for this right. Honour thy father and mother; which is the first commandment with promise; that it may be well with thee, and thou mayest live long on the earth" (**Ephesians 6:1-3**).

Your Obedience To Your Employer Guarantees Reward From God.

"Servants, be obedient to them that are your masters according to the flesh, with fear and trembling, and in singleness of your heart, as unto Christ... Knowing that whatsoever good thing any man doeth, the same shall he receive of the Lord, whether he be bond or free" (**Ephesians 6:5`, 8**).

Your Obedience To Treat Your Employees Fairly Assures Compensation From Your Spiritual Overseer, God.

"And, ye masters, do the same things unto them, forbearing threatening: knowing that your Master also is in heaven; neither is there respect of persons with Him" (**Ephesians 6:9**).

Your Obedience To Make Good Things Happen To Others Will Bring A Blessing From God.

"Withhold not good from them to whom it is due, when it is in the power of thine hand to do it" 1Proverbs 3:27).

The greatest success principle I've ever discovered in my life is—What You Make Happen for Others, God Will Make Happen For You. (**See Ephesians 6:8.**)

Your Obedience To Put On The Whole Armour Of God Guarantees Your Ability To Withstand Through Any Crisis.

"Wherefore take unto you the whole armour of God, that ye may be able to withstand in the evil day, and having done all, to stand" (Ephesians 6:13).

Your Obedience To Keep Your Personal Prayer Appointment With The Holy Spirit, Guarantees Uncommon And Total Joy.

"..In thy presence is fullness of joy; at thy right hand there are pleasures for evermore" (Psalm 16:11b).

David describes the rewards of His presence.

"One thing have I desired of the Lord, that will I seek after; that I may dwell in the house of the Lord all the days of my life, to behold the beauty of the Lord, and to inquire in His temple" (Psalm 27:4).

Your Obedience To Fear The Lord Births The Secrets Of God Within Your Life.

"What man is he that feareth the Lord? Him shall He

teach him the way that He shall choose. His soul shall dwell at ease; and His Seed shall inherit the earth. The secret of the Lord is with them that fear Him; and He will show them His covenant" **(Psalm 25:12- 14).**

Your Obedience To Wait Patiently On The Timing Of God Guarantees The Goodness Of God.

"The Lord is good unto them that wait for Him, to the soul that seeketh Him. It is good that a man should both hope and quietly wait for the salvation of the Lord" **(Lamentations 3:25, 26).**

Your Obedience To Prophetic Authority Will Bring Uncommon Revelation And Blessing.

"Surely the Lord God will do nothing, but He revealeth His secret unto His servants the prophets" (Amos 3:7).

"...Believe in the Lord your God, so shall ye be established; believe His prophets, so shall ye prosper" *(2 Chronicles 20:20b).*

When thousands sneer and laugh and jeer at a man of God speaking prophetically, others walk in that light and explode into uncommon promotion. It is One of the Master Keys to increasing your life—One Thousand Times More.

Your Obedience To Sing, Praise And Worship God Positions God As An Adversary To Deal With Your Enemies And Bring Their Defeat.
"And when he had consulted with the people, he appointed singers unto the Lord that should praise the beauty of holiness, as they went out before the army, and to say, Praise the Lord; for

His mercy endureth for ever. And when they began to sing and to praise, the Lord set ambushments against the children of Ammon, Moab and mount Seir, which were come out against Judah; and they were smitten" (2 Chronicles 20:21,22).

Your Obedience To Pastoral Authority Brings Blessing.
"Obey them that have the rule over you, and submit yourselves: for they watch for your souls, as they that must give account, that they may do it with joy, and not with grief: for that is unprofitable for you" (Hebrews 13:17).

Your Obedience To Sever Wrong Relationship Prevents Tragedy. You see, every act of obedience produces an inevitable reward.
"And have no fellowship with the unfruitful works of darkness, but rather reprove them" (Ephesians 5:11).
Samson was disobedient and lost the status of championship. His eyes were gouged out, and he became the laughingstock of the Philistines. Disobedience is costly. Embarrassing, Humiliating and Unnecessary.
"Be not deceived: evil communications corrupt good manners" (1 Corinthians 15:33).
Your Obedience To Rely Totally On The Word Of God Creates Uncommon Favor
"..But let thine heart keep my commandments: For length of days, and long life, and peace, shall they add to thee. Let not mercy and truth forsake

thee: bind them upon thy neck; and write them upon the table of thine heart: So shalt thou find favour and good understanding in the sight of God and man" (Proverbs 3:1b-4).

Your Obedience to Honor God With The First fruits Of Any Financial Blessing Guarantees Uncommon Financial Prosperity.

"Honour the Lord with thy substance, and the first fruits of all thine increase: so shall thy barns be filled with plenty, and thy presses shall burst out with new wine" (Proverbs 3:9, 10).

Obedience To Stay Humble Toward God And Fear Him In Avoiding Evil Even Affects Your Health.

"Be not wise in thine own eyes: fear the Lord, and depart from evil. It shall be health to thy navel and marrow to thy bones" (Proverbs 3:7, 8).

Your Obedience To Pursue Wisdom As The Principle Focus Of Your Life Guarantees Continuous Joy And Victory.

"Happy is the man that findeth wisdom, and the man that getteth understanding... Her ways are ways of pleasantness, and all her paths are peace. She is a tree of life to them that lay hold upon her: and happy is every one that retaineth her" (Proverbs 3:13, 17, 18).

God Often Permits Adversity To Unlock A Desire To Obey And To Learn His Laws.

"It is good for me that I have been afflicted; that I might learn Thy statutes" (Psalm 119:71).

When You Are At The Place Of Obedience, The Right People Move into your life. When Ruth obediently adapted to the schedule of Naomi, Boaz emerged. When Elijah went to Zarephath, the widow emerged. When Esther obeyed the instructions of Mordecai, the king showed favor.

Provision Is Only Guaranteed At Your Place Of Obedience. Ruth had to be at the place where Boaz could see her. Joseph had to be seen by Pharaoh before he was promoted. Esther had to be seen by the king. It is important to always be at the very place, the job, the company or even the town God wants you. If you are not where God has assigned you, start moving in that direction. Secure counsel from your Mentors, your boss, your family.

Develop a passion for hourly obedience to the Inner Voice of your greatest Advisor and Mentor, the Holy Spirit.

It is the Master Key to the promise of One Thousand Times More.

9

EMBRACE CONSECRATION

Say ye to the righteous, that it shall be well with him,
For they shall eat the fruit of their doings. (Isa. 3:10)

God, without any doubt, is taking us somewhere, to a place of honor, a place of glory, the place of beauty. It's called the place of uncommon fortunes. By divine authority you will surely get there.

When the Lord shall build up Zion, he shall appear in his glory. (Psa. 102:16)

What is this saying?

That is, God will come when Zion has taken her full and right position. Jesus will be here after Zion has fully taken her position in destiny. After she has taken over on the earth, according to God's word.

Then all nations shall flow unto her (Isa. 2:2)

That of course is talking about the church.

God is preparing us for that ultimate, so that the sons of God will take over the affairs of life on this earth.

You won't miss your place in it!

Every plan of God has a foundation. If you don't understand the foundation, you will suffer frustration. That's what **Psalm 11:3** makes us understand:

If the foundations be destroyed, what can the righteous do?

So every plan and purpose of God has its foundation, and as we embark on this adventure into the realms of glory and honor it is necessary for us to properly examine the foundation for the Jesus kind of glory and honor so we won't be building on sand.

 2 Timothy 2:19 tells us:

Nevertheless the foundation of God standeth sure, having this seal; The Lord knoweth them that are his. And let everyone that nameth the name of Christ depart from iniquity.

We need to understand that every one of God's provisions for man has this as its foundation

"Depart from iniquity".

By God i am going to show you truths from the Holy

Scriptures that will help you to appreciate this fact, so that the subsequent teachings can be maximally profitable to you.

The Word of God provides a four-dimensional ministry to us. Thus:

'' All scripture is giving by the inspiration of God, and is profitable for DOCTRINE, for REPROOF, for CORRECTION, for INSTRUCTION in RIGHTEOUSNESS'' **2 Timothy 3:16**

Sir. If this is out of place the principles won't work, adjustments will not produce either. But when the foundation is in place, every other thing keeps working.

The foundation is crucial to every structure. So as we proceed to unravel the mystery of glory structured in this book we need good understanding.

The mother of poverty.

And the Lord God called unto Adam and said unto him. Where art thou?

And he said I heard thy voice in the garden, and I **was afraid because I was naked: and I hid myself. Genesis 3:9-10**

Man was put in the garden.

And the Lord God took the man and put him into the Garden of Eden to dress it and to keep it.

And the Lord commanded the man, saying, of every tree of the garden thou mayest freely eat:

But of the tree of the knowledge of good and evil, thou shalt not eat: for the day thou eatest thereof, thou shalt surely die.   **Genesis 2:15-17**

But he messed up big time

And when the woman saw that the tree was good for food, and that it was pleasant to the eyes, and a tree to be desired to make one wise, she took of the fruit thereof, and did eat, and gave also unto her husband with her; and he did eat. And the eyes of them both were opened; and they sewed fig leaves together, and made themselves aprons. **Genesis 3:6-7**

The immediate effect of man's fall was nakedness. He was stripped of honor, rest and dignity as a result of sin.

Therefore, sin is the mother of poverty! Sin striped man naked! Struggle, Poverty and shame arrived upon man right there in the garden, seconding the arrival of sin.

Therefore, the Lord God sent him forth from the garden, to till the ground from whence he was taken.

So he drove out the man; and he placed at the east of the Garden of Eden, Cherubim's, and a flaming sword which turned every way to keep the way of the tree of life. **Genesis 3:23-24**

This was where all of man's depravity, struggle, labor, and toiling began.

Sin sent man out of plenty into scarcity, out of favor into

labor, out of luxury into penury, out of manifestation to expectation. Sin drove man out of luxury and glory into the wilderness of want and abject lack.

Sir. It was sin that drove man out of the garden into a perpetual wilderness experience not the serpent, not God but sin.

Therefore, we can conclude by saying that, at the root of every form of human calamity, paucity, poverty, depravity, futility, and loss of indemnity is sin.

Give Up Sin!!

Nevertheless the foundation of God standeth sure, having this seal; The Lord knoweth them that are his. And let everyone that nameth the name of Christ depart from iniquity. **2 Timothy 2:19**

Until you step out of sin you cannot experience the 1,000 times more reality.

This is the foundation for kingdom prosperity.

If you return to the Almighty, thou shalt be built up; thou shalt put away iniquity far from thy tabernacles.

Then shalt thou lay-up gold as dust and the gold of Ophir as the stones of the brooks. **Job 22:23-24**

When you return to the Almighty and separate yourself from sin, then you become a candidate for the delivery of glory and virtue.

The foundation has not changed. Departure from sin is not an option, it's an imperative stipulate. It is what guarantees your access into the promise. Until you depart you will never be part of the massive budget, you won't ever see the reality of this promise no matter what method you use.

If you enjoy sin, you will never experience the materialization of the promise of glory and virtue as it is thus; A MYSTERY (secret). And his secrets are not for any how people but rather for   *" those who fear him "* *as* in (**Psa. 25:14**)

Who will God unveil this mysteries or secrets to? Of course, those who fear him.

Thus; The fear of God is what qualifies your access into the MYSTERY OF 1,000 MORE which guarantees your sweat less triumph in all areas of life.... it was on the same secrets that Job traded as he said;

I washed my steps with butter, and the rock poured me out rivers of oil. **Job.29:6**

You must as a matter of urgency and necessity eschew evil. Go after holiness. Love righteousness, hate wickedness and then you can grasp the revelation of this mysteries which will in turn enhance the delivery of this promise into your life.

Get back to Eden.

For the Lord shall comfort Zion; he will comfort all her waste places; he will make her wilderness like Eden, and her desert like the garden of the Lord; Joy and gladness shall be found therein, thanksgiving, and the voice of melody. **Isa. 51:3**

God is saying here, *"hearken unto me all ye who follow*

after righteousness" *I* am taking you back to Eden; that is why i am cleaning you up. You are the seed of the second Adam. It is your heritage to get back to Eden. Keep following righteousness, you will soon get there. It is your destination. Even the place of glory. For if God be for us, who can be against us.

Purity begat plenty.

Righteousness exalts a nation but sin is a reproach.Prov.14:34

 As we proceed on this journey, in a proffer to grasp these mysteries as the fundamentals for these promises. It has its roots on Integrity. Kingdom purity is what gives birth to Kingdom plenty.

Consecration is your first step into Kingdom of God; God will give your life balance when you are consecrated to Him.

Joseph said, he feared God, and even in prison he prospered, because he was on the right frequency. Job was a man that feared God, a perfect man, and he became the greatest in the East.

Crookedness never earns anyone a future!

Wealth gotten by vanity shall be diminished; But he that gathereth by labour shall increase. **Proverbs 13:11**

There is a place of no want, a place of no lack, but access to that becomes possible after you have taken a deliberate responsibility to turn away from iniquity and purge yourself. Then will God rescue you from the wilderness life into the Eden life experience.

Seed sowing or planting does not guarantee automatic prosperity. No! It's your work with God. As God himself prospered Abraham yet he said to him

''*Walk before me and be thou perfect*'' **Gen. 17:1**

Friends, I submit to you that the covenant is not a claim, it is a walk!

Enoch walked with God and was not, because God took him. And before he was translated, he had this testimony that he pleased God. **(Gen. 5:24), (Heb. 1:5)**

God took him, so he did not see dead. I dare you to walk with God and see how he will take you into royalty.

Purity is a lifetime adventure. To be tired of purity is to be tired of plenty.

Embrace and practice holiness!

But refuse profane and old wives' fables and exercise thy self rather unto godliness. **1 Tim. 4:7**

I call Godliness ''**God-likeness**''. God's predominant nature is holiness.

Rev. 4:8 says; *Holy, Holy, Holy is the Lord almighty.*

So, there is no Godlikeness without holiness being embraced and practiced. Godliness is profitable unto all things. So, purity has earthly values!

There is a place of no lack on this earth, and it is only guaranteed when you live a sin-free life. God is saying, if

I chased man out of Eden because of sin, no man will have a test of the reality of Eden while in sin. Until you are set for righteousness, Eden will perpetually remain a mirage to you. It will never be in view.

1 Tim. 6:6, 11 says;

But Godliness and contentment is great gain But thou oh man of God, flee this things; and follow after righteousness, godliness, faith, love, patience, meekness.

Great gain means; Glory and honor (Great prosperity). Follow righteousness, follow Godliness, and follow after faith, love, patience and meekness, and you shall inherit the earth. Follow all these and you will surely enjoy plenty, beyond what anybody can lay hold on with struggles and efforts.

Purity begets plenty! With indemnity!! Iniquity begets paucity, poverty, calamity, futility and scarcity. If you are not financially straight, you will suffer and die in wretchedness! So, awake to righteousness and stop playing games and stop cheating men. It takes financial sanity to enjoy financial plenty; it takes financial integrity to enjoy financial plenty with indemnity.

May God help you to remain financially straight so you can be qualified for royalty, Amen.

Nothing beautifies like holiness. *In the beauty of holiness, in the womb of the morning: thou hath the dew of thy youth* **(Psalm.110:3).**

Nothing dignifies like integrity. *The integrity of the upright shall preserve him. (Proverbs 11:3)*

Nothing uplifts like uprightness. *His seed shall be mighty upon the earth; the generation of the upright shall be blessed. (Psalm 112:2)*

Nothing flourishes like righteousness. *The righteous shall flourish like the palm tree; he shall grow up like the cedar in Lebanon. (Psalm 92:12)*

Nothing is as colorful as consecration. *If any purges himself of this thing, he shall be a vessel unto honour.* **(2 Timothy 2:19-21)**

Nothing prospers like purity.

It is a satanic oppression to think purity equals poverty! The purest place in the universe is also the wealthiest place, i.e., Heaven. Heaven is the purest place in the whole of creation and as well the wealthiest place, the streets are paved with pure gold. It was sin remember that brought nakedness. Holiness makes beautiful.

Glory and honor promise is not for fools

Proverbs 1:32 says, *"The prosperity of fools shall destroy them"*

Fools make mockery of sin. **Proverbs 14:9 say,** *"fools make a mock at sin:* **but among the righteous there is favour"**

Of sin, they say, it does not matter, it is normal, everybody is doing it.

Thus, the God of all knowledge denies them uncommon increase as it has the propensity of destroying them, he keeps these promise from them because they are fools.

It is cheap to connect purity to plenty. God is the purest and the wealthiest. He said,

"The silver is mine and the gold is mine"

David the Psalmist of Israel said,

"The earth is the Lord's and the fullness thereof" **God the holiest of all** is the God of all reaches and wealth.

Sir. You must accept this fact as I put it to you that plenty is the bye product of purity.

Personal purity guarantees personal plenty.   And impurity is the grand enemy of plenty.

Iniquity is the reason why many have preached and prophesied prosperity and many can quote the scriptures on this subject but only a few have handled it as a reality.

My dear reader, your heart and habits go a long way in your desire for this promise. But if you can put your heart in line with God, and your heart under covenant control, then you can be sure that this promise will certainly become a reality in your life.

I am happy for you today because you have probably identified an area of human weakness where the devil has been the master in your life, right now begin to plead the blood of Jesus against that satanic manipulation. That anger, that malice, evil eye, envy, etc.

When sin goes, lack dies!

Giving will never be equal to the materialization of prosperity until the foundation is in place. Sir. You can give all you want but you will never get to see the promise. This promise is traceable to first, victory over sin. Your giving remains a mere philanthropic adventure until you return to God in truth and variety.

Two great prosperity scriptures make this clear;

.....Return unto me and i will return unto you..............**Malachi 3:7**

.....*if thou return to the almighty, thou shalt be built up, thou shalt put away iniquity far from thy tabernacles. Then shalt thou lay-up gold as dust and the gold of ophire as the stones of the brooks. Yea, the almighty shalt be thy defense, and thou shalt have plenty of silver.* Job 22:23-25

This promise begins as we return. The wilderness is the portion of sinners because God is angry with sinners every day.

If only you will clean up, all your seed sown that are even dying will come back to life.

Righteousness enthrones! It causes to flourish! It dignifies! It beautifies!

Joseph refused sin. If you don't refuse sin, you will soon become a refuse. If Joseph had not refused sin, he would have become a lifelong refuse in the house of Potiphar and Egypt by extension. **(Genesis 41:38-44)**

Of Daniel, he transcended all his persecutors and became their head, because an excellent spirit was found in him. He was known with his God. It is time for you to be known with your God too. May you prefer to be cheated than to cheat someone.

Be awake, we are serving a heavenly banker, and a heavenly father, God cannot be in need. He is not in need of your money! I must drum this truth into you very well.

God said in

Proverbs 23:26. *My Son, give me your heart.*

A departure from iniquity and a return home is the foundation for the promise of prosperity. So long as the prodigal son remained away, he remained naked and alienated from his father's coverage. But his return home ended his lifetime nakedness. He was clothed into a celebrity.

You will not suffer any more! Your nakedness has come to an end, by divine authority.

Sin is a destroyer, not a friend. You must fight it with all your being. Your future is tied to sinlessness. The true riches of God are for faithful stewards. Go for righteousness as it equals fruitfulness. There is a great future in purity, let's go for it head long. Iniquity is a destroyer, let's destroy it.

God is taking you from the wilderness of lack and want where you have been tilling and toiling back to Eden. From today, i speak by divine authority that because you have this book, all your days of hardship, labor, shame, embarrassment, and humiliation have come to an end

Consecration is imperative, you won't be GIFTED and STRANDED.

10

SUBSCRIBE TO DELIGENCE

Proverbs 22:29 *"Seest thou a man diligent in his business? He shall stand before kings; he shall not stand before mean men."*

My friend, Gift is not enough, talent is not enough you must settle for diligence if your purpose is fulfilled.

Diligence can be defined as doing something with care and effort. Not just doing it but doing it with care and effort. Over the years I have seen many hardworking and scripture-quoting Christians making no form of headway. I will not shy away from telling you that I was equally a victim of this heartache.

But thank God I came out by reason of insight. Please note that we win in life by discoveries. Your degree of light determines the brightness of your life. It is your depth that determines your height in life.

I found out that hard work does not always culminate in success or excellence. Even in some cases hard work is only an extension of existing hardship. I found out that I need a strategy in all my work and dealings. The scripture clearly says the labor of the fool wearies all of them because he does not KNOW HOW to get to the city. So, strategy is the HOW TO, and I pray that you will not run in vain.

To every work there is a skill required and behind every excellent performance is strategic work and organized rhythm. After I made this discovery, I began to sit down and seek God's face and ask Him for the strategy required to accomplish whatever He shows or lays in my heart.

Strategy is a set out plan in achieving a major goal. If you don't know where you are going you will never know when you arrive there. I want to encourage you that regardless of your vision and the sincerity of your desire you will suffer unnecessary pain if you don't have a plan and strategic approach to achieving your goals. It is not enough to have a goal and desire great things, but you also need to sit down first and count the pros and cons of your desired goal. Have a plan in your head and the Holy Spirit in your heart.

You must have established a set plan and a reasonable one because if you have not been on level 1 and you now set a goal for level 30 you are creating unrealistic and apparently unachievable goals and wasting your time. For example, a man that has not successfully lived by faith with a job how would he live by faith without a job? He is only fooling himself; time will prove him wrong.

After you have set out a reasonable plan of action then you need to unleash your energy to work as hard as you can and with God's supernatural support you will succeed, not just because you are a child of God but a diligent and wise child. I see you work diligently and achieve excellent results in all you do in Jesus mighty name!

11

PURSUE EXCELLENCE

Proverbs 12:26 – *The righteous is more excellent than his neighbour: but the way of the wicked seduceth them.*

Daniel 6:3 – *Then this Daniel was preferred above the presidents and princes, because an excellent spirit was in him; and the king thought to set him over the whole realm.*

Excellence is a spirit and for everyone who is in Christ, excellence is given. It comes with the redemption package. The Bible declares that Jesus obtained a more excellent ministry which is steered by an even more excellent Spirit. The Bible went further to say, "...as He is, so are we in this world," 1 John 4:17. This implies that we share in the same ministry of excellence with Christ! Glory! Alleluia! We have the excellent spirit.

A great preacher once said, "You do not know your worth that's why you cannot carry your weight!"

When we realize that the same Spirit which distinguished Daniel has been given to us under a better covenant and arrangement, then our outlook to life takes an upturn. Excellence is a spiritual treasure locked away in the chest of our human spirit and we need to go on an adventure to unlock it.

The most glaring effect of excellence in the life of Daniel and anyone for that matter is promotion! Excellence as defined by the Spirit churns out favor in the life of them that have it. You see, you cannot be promoted if you have not been favored and the more robust your promotion is, the greater is the substance called excellence that is at work in your life.

It is essential that you know that Supernatural excellence is a substance that is created by the operation of the Holy Spirit in the life of the believer. However, the manifestation of it lies in the self determination of the believer. In other words, it is a choice. After all, the journey of Daniel and his friends into stardom began when Daniel and his circle of friends determined and decided that they were not going to defile themselves with the king's meat. This is very instructive as an example to those who seek to experience the unhindered flow of excellence in their lives. You must decide before excellence can be deployed in your life! Daniel chose to be excellent, and we read about how he was preferred.

While the seed of excellence is undeniably resident within you, you must fan it to flame through the agency of spirited determination placed with an array of spiritual activities like prayer, confession, and principled lifestyle just like Daniel and his friends did in Bible times. When these happen, your life will take a most radiant dimension and your God will turn you into a celebrity. O yes! You become a celebrity because the spirit of excellence brings you out of the shadows and turns the spotlight on you while bringing glory to the name of your God. This was the testimony of Daniel.

Remember, excellence is a spirit, but it needs a yielded vessel through which it can manifest. It is true that we are excellent by redemption, but we manifest excellence by yielding to the movement of the Holy Spirit in our life. Otherwise, life will continue to appear as a string of trials and errors which is not a reflection of a supernaturally driven life.

As we journey further in this life, it is my firm conviction that the Holy Spirit will raise the standard of our lives as He continues to pump more substance of excellence into our existence, and we shall all testify.

12

PLUG INTO PRAYER POWER

F.B. Meyer, the author of the great little book, The Secret of Guidance said, "The great tragedy of life is not unanswered prayer, but un-offered prayer."

Instead of it being something we do every day, like breathing, eating and walking and talking, it seems to have become like that little glass covered box on the wall that says, "break in case of emergency." It is true that so very often we associate prayer with crises in our life.

I heard a story the other day of a man who encountered a bit of trouble while flying his little airplane. He called the control tower and said, "Pilot to tower, I'm 300 miles from the airport, six hundred feet above the ground, and I'm out of fuel. I am descending rapidly. Please advise. Over." "Tower to pilot," the dispatcher began, "Repeat after me: "Our Father Who art in heaven...'"

Prayer is, for the most part, an untapped resource, an unexplored continent where untold treasure remains to be unearthed. It is talked about more than anything else and practiced less than anything else. And yet, for the believer it remains one of the greatest gifts our Lord has given us outside of salvation.

In 1952, Albert Einstein was delivering a lecture on the campus of Princeton University. A doctoral student asked the famous scientist "What is there left in the world for original dissertation research?" With considerate thought and profundity Einstein replied, "Find out about prayer. Somebody must find out about prayer."

Paul was somebody who understood prayer and its power. Prayer was a part of Paul's life, and he took it for granted that it would be a part of the life of every Christian. You cannot really be a good Christian and not pray, just like you cannot have a good marriage if you don't talk to your wife. You can be a Christian and not pray, just like you can be married and not

talk to your wife. But in both circumstances, you will be miserable. Prayer is the pipeline of communication between God and His people, between God and those who love Him.

I. Pray with persistence

Paul begins by saying, ***"Devote yourselves to prayer," (NASB) or "Continue earnestly in prayer***," (NKJV). In the original language it says, "continue steadfastly in prayer." The word translated, "continue steadfastly," is one word in the original language. It can be translated, "persist in, adhere firmly to, or remain devoted to or to give unremitting care to." It carries with it the idea of dedication. Of the ten times it is used in the New Testament four of them have to do with being devoted to prayer. It is a very powerful word and in this verse is given as an imperative, or a command. In other words, persistence in prayer is not an option for the Christian it is an order from the Lord Himself.

Two of the most instructive parables Jesus ever told on prayer, one in Luke 18 and the other in Luke 11, both have to do with being persistent and not giving up in prayer.

Luke 18:1 says, "Now He was telling them a parable to show them that at all times they ought to pray and not to lose heart."

Luke 11:9 is where we find the promise that says, "ask and it shall be given to you; seek and you shall find; knock and it shall be opened to you." Each of those verbs are in the present tense, active voice and could be translated, "keep on asking, keep on seeking, keep on knocking." Jesus does not want us to give up in prayer, He instructs us to be persistent.

Now there is a difference between a persistent prayer and a long prayer. A person who is persistent in prayer does not necessarily have to pray for a long time. Persistence means not giving up.

Some people give up easy, they quit because they say they don't feel like praying, the joy is gone, the feeling is gone. But we are not to live by our feelings but to live by the commandments of our Lord who tells us to pray without ceasing.

George Muller, known as one of the greatest prayer warriors of all times had this to say about persistence in prayer"

"It is a common temptation of Satan to make us give up the reading of the Word and prayer when our enjoyment is gone; as if it were of no use to read the scriptures when we do not enjoy them, and as if it were no use to pray when we have no spirit of prayer. The truth is that, to enjoy the Word, we ought to continue to read it, and the way to obtain a spirit of prayer is to continue praying. The less we read the Word of God, the less we desire to read it, and the less we pray, the less we desire to pray."

Be persistent in prayer.

II. Pray with passion

If you are persistent in something, it stands to reason that you are to be passionate about it. In fact, Paul says we should be vigilant or be watchful; it is the opposite of slothfulness. This describes passionate prayer.

Jesus was passionate about His prayer life; it was something He was always doing.

S.D. Gordon in his book, Quiet Talks on Prayer, says

How much prayer meant to Jesus! It was not only his regular habit, but his resort in every emergency, however slight or serious. When perplexed he prayed. When hard pressed by work he prayed. When hungry for fellowship he found it in prayer. He chose his associates and received his messages upon his knees. If tempted, he prayed. If criticized, he prayed. If fatigued in body or wearied in spirit, he had recourse to his one unfailing habit of prayer. Prayer brought him unmeasured power at the beginning and kept the flow unbroken and undiminished. There was no emergency, no difficulty, no necessity, no temptation that would not yield to prayer.

And every time we see Jesus praying, He was praying with passion.

In Luke 3:1 at His Baptism - while He was praying the heaven was opened. Passionate prayer opens Heaven.

In Luke 6:12 before He called His disciples - He spent the whole night in prayer. Passionate prayer gives direction.

In Luke 9:29 at His transfiguration - And while He was praying, the appearance of His face became different, and His clothing became white and gleaming. Passionate prayer enables us to experience the glory of the Father.

In John 17 in His high priestly prayer - Passionate prayer impacts the lives of others.

In Matthew 26:39 in the Garden of Gethsemane - It is only through passionate prayer that we can pour out our hearts to God.

In Luke 23:24 as He hung on the cross - a life that is lived in passionate prayer will enable us to maintain that spirit, even in the most difficult of circumstances.

Jesus always prayed with passion, because He knew Who it was He was talking to and He knew that prayer to the Father is a powerful thing and not something to take lightly and glibly.

Prayer from the heart, that's what passionate prayer is, it is prayer from the heart not just from the head.

That is how He taught us to pray, not only through His example, but specifically through His teaching Look in Matthew 6:7, in the Sermon on the Mount as Jesus instructs on prayer. It is here that we find the Lord's prayer. But just before the Lord's prayer what does He say?

"When you pray, do not use meaningless repetition as the Gentiles do."

(Jews around the world may now send prayers via fax to the Wailing Wall)

What has happened to the Lord's Prayer? People repeat it as if it were magic mantra that will bless them or move God to hear them. What they are doing with it is exactly what He was instructing us not to do with it. The gentiles, when they prayed tried, through their religious repetitions, with their chants and their mantras to call forth or impress their Gods. That is not what you do when you are in a relationship.

You don't tell your wife. "I love you, oh I really love you and I just wanted to tell you today that I love you, I'm so glad that I just have this time to just say I love you. Please feed the children, please clean the house and may all go well with you." Amen

James 5:16 says, "The effective, fervent prayer of a righteous man can accomplish much."

III. Pray with thankfulness

Paul never fails to mention it.

Ephesians 5:20 tells us that thanksgiving is the natural result of being filled with and walking under the influence of the Holy Spirit.

Philippians 4:6 tells us to be anxious for nothing but in everything we should pray, giving thanks as we make our petitions known to God.

1 Thessalonians 5:18 tells us that giving thanks at all times is God's will for us in Christ Jesus.

Colossians 3:17 says that as believers everything

we say or do should be done in the name of the Lord Jesus as we give thanks to Him.

1 Timothy 4:4 - says that food and marriage are good things given to us by God and are to be received with thanksgiving and gratitude.

Expressing gratitude does several things:

It articulates dependence

It demonstrates relationship

It communicates gratitude - proper attitudes

It generates humility

IV. Pray, making intercession

Intercessory prayer is basically praying for others, it is praying for God's will to be done in the lives of other people.

Intercessory prayers characterized the prayer life of Jesus.

In Isaiah 53:12 the Bible says, He Himself bore the sins of many and, interceded for the transgressors."

Luke 22:23 Jesus tells Peter, "I have prayed for you, that your faith may not fail;"

Luke 23:34 on the cross, Jesus was praying for others when He said, "Father forgive them for they do not know what they are doing."

John 14:15 Jesus interceded for us, asking the Father to send the Holy Spirit

John 17:19 He prayed for us, the church, in His High Priestly prayer. Listen to the intercessory nature of this prayer, "I ask on their behalf; I do not ask on behalf of the world, but of those whom Thou has given Me . . . "

Romans 8:34 tells us that Jesus is seated at the right hand of the Father, making intercession for us.

And Hebrews 7:25 says, "Hence, also, He is able to save forever those who draw near to God through Him, since He always lives to make intercession for them."

Jesus prayed intercessory prayers; He was ever praying for others.

Understanding the power of Prayer, Paul wanted to be sure the Colossian Christians understood what it was they were to pray for. He wanted them to pray with a specific purpose. He wanted them to pray for him, asking God to open a door so that they could speak the gospel. It was the gospel that Paul lived for, it was the preaching of the gospel that had landed Paul in prison, it was the preaching of the gospel that was ever on the forefront of Paul's mind. You see, Paul wanted God's kingdom to expand. Like Jesus, he was concerned about others, about their souls, their salvation, and their sanctification.

It is instructive to note that Paul is not asking them to pray for his legal situation or that he would be released from prison. He is asking them to pray that he will have the opportunity to lead someone to Christ.

Paul wanted their prayers to be in accordance with God's will not simply after the greedy desires of someone living for this world.

Paul was always concerned with doing the will of God. How many of our prayers are directed at the expansion of His eternal kingdom rather than the expansion of our petty kingdoms? If you were able to chronicle your prayers, knowing how much time you spent praying for different things, how much of your time would be spent praying for your family, for their health, for the health and well-being of your loved ones, compared to how much time you were praying for the lost who are headed to hell?

Intercessory prayer changes things.

Howard Hendricks, who for years taught at the Dallas Theological Seminary and pastored in the area shared this story. He said:

Years ago, in a church in Dallas we were having trouble finding a teacher for a junior high boy's class. The list of prospects had only one name -- and when they told me who it was, I said, "You've got to be kidding." But I couldn't have been more wrong about that young man. He took the class and revolutionized it.

I was so impressed I invited him to my home for lunch and asked him the secret of his success. He pulled out a little black book. On each page he had a small picture of one of the boys, and under the boy's name were comments like "having trouble in arithmetic," or "comes to church against parents' wishes," or "would like to be a missionary someday but doesn't think he has what it takes."

"I pray over those pages every day," he said, "and I can hardly wait to come to church each Sunday to see what God has been doing in their lives."

You see, when you pray for others, when you pray for God's work to be done, for His will to be accomplished, He will begin to use you and grow you in ways that will astonish those around you. Sometimes I think we do not become what God wants us to become, because we are too focused on ourselves and not on others. It is when we pray for others that we will become more like Jesus, and as we become more like Jesus God will grow us more, show us more, and use us more. We must pray for others.

Four things that happen when we pray:

1. Prayer internalizes the burden

It deepens our ownership of the burden and our partnership with God. As we pray, we begin to become aware of how God might us to answer the prayer, how He might involve us in ways we had not theretofore foreseen.

2. Prayer forces us to wait

Part of prayer is always waiting for God. God has

three answers to prayers: Yes, no and wait. Yes and no are no-brainers. But wait, that is tough. John MacArthur says: "There is a tension between boldness and waiting on God's will. That tension is resolved by being persistent yet accepting God's answer when it finally comes." Instead of getting frustrated that God is not on our schedule, prayer forces us to be on God's timetable.

3. Prayer opens our spiritual eyes

It enables us to get in touch with what God is doing and how He is doing it.

In II Kings 6 you may recall the story of when the Army of Israel was surrounded by their enemies and Elijah's servant got nervous. Verses 15-17 say

Now when the attendant of the man of God had risen early and gone out, behold, an army with horses and chariots was circling the city. And his servant said to him, "Alas, my master! What shall we do?" 16So he answered, "Do not fear, for those who are with us are more than those who are with them." 17Then Elisha prayed and said, "O LORD, I pray, open his eyes that he may see." And the LORD opened the servant's eyes and he saw; and behold, the mountain was full of horses and chariots of fire all around Elisha.

Prayer opens our eyes, enabling us to see what God is doing, to see things we are blinded to without prayer. That's because prayer is communication. We speak to God, God answers us, speaking to us, showing us.

Adjustment, alignment, setting our thoughts, emotions, actions.

4. Prayer enables us to move forward

Prayer engages God, enables God's people, and enlarges His kingdom. Jesus said, "without Me, you can do nothing." Once we have prayed, we are ready to do anything, until we have prayed we can do nothing, but once we

have prayed we can accomplish anything.

What does your prayer life look like this morning? Are you persistent in prayer? Are your prayers passionate or are they perfunctory? Are they filled with intensity and fervor or are they weak, timid, and lacking faith? What about gratitude? How much time have you spent thanking God for all He has done for you? And who are you praying for? Is there anyone in your life that you are praying will get saved? Is there a burden on your heart to see God's kingdom expand, to see His will done? Of no, start today.

Prayer is necessary for a life of glory and total Dominion.

Men will remain gifted but stranded until they subscribe to prayer.

ABOUT THE AUTHOR

Johnny is president of the J Riley Consultant Group, LLC. He is also president and CEO of Bridging the GAPS Ministries International a global non-profit focused on leaders and leadership development. He is the author of Crabology, From The Heart, From The Heart Too, and the last week of Jesus' Life.

He speaks in conferences annually all over the world. The locations he has spoken in are Malawi, Zimbabwe, Johannesburg, South Africa; Jos Plateau State, Nigeria; Abuja, Nigeria, West Africa; Lagos State, Nigeria; Honduras; Mexico; and Guatemala. He also currently serves as an advisory to many African and Central America counties. Recently he was selected by the organization founded by Dr. Martin Luther King Jr., the Southern Christian Leadership Conference to speak at the 50th Anniversary of the March on Washington in Washington   DC.